THE

GOOD HOUSEKEEPING

HOSTESS

ENTERTAINMENTS FOR ALL SEASONS
AND OCCASIONS, DESCRIBED IN DETAIL BY A GROUP
OF ACCOMPLISHED ENTERTAINERS

ALSO

THE COMPLETE RULES OF ETIQUETTE AND SOCIAL
OBSERVANCE FOR THE HOSTESS

HEARST BOOKS
A Division of Sterling Publishing Co., Inc.
New York

ORIGINALLY PUBLISHED AND COPYRIGHTED IN 1904
by The Phelps Publishing Co.

Published by Hearst Books
A Division of Sterling Publishing Co., Inc.
387 Park Avenue South, New York, NY 10016

www.goodhousekeeping.com

Distributed in Canada by Sterling Publishing
c/o Canadian Manda Group, One Atlantic Avenue,
Suite 105 Toronto, Ontario, Canada M6K 3E7
Distributed in Australia by
Capricorn Link (Australia) Pty. Ltd.
P.O. Box 704, Windsor, NSW 2756 Australia

Manufactured in China

10 9 8 7 6 5 4 3 2 1

ISBN 1-58816-250-8

TABLE OF CONTENTS

SOCIAL LIFE

SOCIAL LIFE

Sundry Obligations

IT sometimes happens in our experience that though we possess many beautiful and valuable bits of information, we lack that very one for which we have immediate need, and like the lady who glories in nine rose point berthas and perforce remains away from the horse show for want of linen collar and cuffs, we may know quite glibly that the nation's chief in far-away Washington is addressed as His Excellency, and yet pucker our brows in vain bewilderment as to whether plain little next-door Lucy is our dear Mrs. Gray or simply dear Lucy since she came home from the honeymoon.

Perhaps it will help a little if we remember that all conventions are in their final analysis dictated by the heart and based on the golden rule. They may have been cut long ago at some grand court, and dried through usage among the gentlefolk of many lands, and yet they are less arbitrary than would seem at first thought. Rules of etiquette have always been equally binding on all members of the set which uses them, and as my lady is sometimes guest and on other occasions hostess, it would plainly be but natural for her to advocate the least irksome duty for each class; besides which is the fact that truly well-bred people regulate their conduct by kindly feeling for each other.

To be sure there are the fads which crop up from year to year, and the improper use of forks and finger bowls has been made such a bogie that many a woman, on her way to a large dinner, trembles at thought of the ordeal before her.   But no lady need really fear. Table etiquette, like all the rest, is primarily to protect us from unpleasing spectacles; and it is by no means impossible for a gentlewoman to handle her asparagus in an old-fashioned manner without losing caste, while the person next her conforms to the fad of the day and yet offends by a too-evident enjoyment of her salad.

If, then, you are not sure as to the exact require- ment in certain social obligations, and have no way of finding out, do the thing you would consider graceful and kind were you in the position of the other person concerned; and above all things, keep on your face the calm smile of self-possession, which goes so far to prove that you know what you are about.

Issuing and Receiving Invitations

Formal intercourse with our kind is regulated by old customs which are amended from time to time.   If you are the entertainer and set out to be ceremonious then put yourself into the hands of the best stationer you can afford, and take his word for the correctness of your invitations.

Strictly speaking, a handsome engraved invitation presupposes an entertainment of equal grandeur; and you may well hesitate and consider, before issuing such, whether your purse will permit you to fulfill what would seem to be the promise of the message. In large formal functions you must probably have aid from the caterer and the florist as well as the stationer; in which case you will almost be a guest in your own house, and must certainly betray no care of cooking or serving; in fact, you must guard against flurry in even the simplest hospitality.

Outside of the large centers of fashion the average American woman has little time, or indeed taste, for strictly formal functions; but throughout the land there blossoms a love for social meeting with one's friends, and never was there a time in our history when happy little circles and gatherings flourished as now.

The invitations for less formal entertainments may be written in conventional third-person wording, following the form of the engraved card. It is more common, however, when your intention is to gather together a party of friends for real pleasure, to be committed to nothing more conventional than good paper and ink, a fair penmanship (that the guests come not on Tuesday when your cook's orders are for two days later), and a respect for the age and the idiosyncrasies of the spelling book. The letters R. S. V. P., and even the later English form of requesting an answer to an invitation, have gone out of fashion; since the rule of reply is supposed to be an understood thing.

To the receiver of invitations the rule of reply is comparatively simple: You follow the lead of the person who has invited you. If the invitation is formally worded in the third person, your reply is similarly worded; and if a personal note bids you to a friend's house, you answer in an unconventional note.

Invitations for receptions, ceremonious weddings, teas where many people are to be present, and all entertainments where the crowd would have to be provided for in any case, and your absence could not cause inconvenience, require no acknowledgment. If you go (except in case of church weddings) you leave a card, and if you do not attend you send your card, enclosed in an envelope, and preferably by messenger to be delivered during the entertainment.

Invitations to dinners, breakfasts, luncheons, the opera, and in fact all entertainments where special place is to be kept for you, must be answered immediately. This is one of the most rigid rules of good breeding, since it is easily understood that no hostess can give her mind calmly to preparation until she has her list of guests complete. If you doubt your ability to attend you must decline at once and give your friend the opportunity to ask someone else. Once made, an engagement may be properly broken for but one cause —outside of illness or grave trouble—namely a conflicting invitation from the President of these United States, and did we observe this rule there would be few chagrined or slighted hostesses in most parts of the country.

In declining invitations it is always more courteous to give your reason, though of course this is not possible in all cases.

In a general way it may be said that every invitation, whether accepted or not, requires a call upon the hostess within two or three weeks after the entertainment; but a breach in the case of general receptions or teas would be more easily forgiven than after dinners, luncheons (any feast where you have eaten at a place assigned specially to you), and those functions whose *raison d'etre* is to introduce a debutante or to honor some particular person or occasion.

Cards

It will not be amiss in closing this chapter on general matters of etiquette, to mention that small, but like the hairpin, indispensable aid to civilization, the visiting card. As with engraved invitations, you must advise with the stationer about size, thickness and type, for these things vary from season to season; though it is safe to say that a neat inconspicuous lettering, either Old English or script, is always in good taste. Initials are tabooed, the full name being always engraved on the card. If, as happens in many a home of the best culture, the hostess herself opens the door, you lay the cards quietly on some table when you rise to leave, one card for each lady of the household, whether you have seen them all or not. If there is a maid or a man servant, you put your bits of pasteboard into the salver offered you for that purpose; and for the sake of those unconventional souls who are not afraid to approach a friend's door because cards have been forgotten, we can only rejoice that all servants are not as zealous as the maid who half shut the door in a lady's face, and said through the narrow crack: "No one gets into this house without a proper ticket."

The visiting card may be used as invitation to teas and afternoon receptions by having the hour and date written in the lower left-hand corner; and it may carry messages of congratulation, condolence, or greeting with gifts, written on the back and signed with name or initials; but it is never used to carry thanks for any courtesy, in which case a note must be written.

Finally, it will bear repetition that conventionalities are based on a kindly desire to meet our fellows on common ground, where all may be at ease, and where none is required to give up all individual characteristics, but only to conform to those rules which are a necessity in any body of men and women.

SPECIAL OCCASIONS

The Christening

My lady first meets the friends of her family when they are bidden to gather for her christening, or, in case that ceremony be not a part of her inheritance, she may be introduced at an old-time caudle party. Except for the religious service in the former, these two functions are practically the same, and on either occasion it is the most intimate of all the family feasts, only those people you really care for being honored with the engraved cards, or the notes asking their presence.

The sponsors are requested by special note, or verbally, to act in that capacity, and tradition has it that the honor is prettily thanked with a gift of silver, a cup or porringer, or perhaps a spoon, for the infant. Other guests may send flowers to the mother, or gifts to the baby, though neither is obligatory.

The hour is chosen according to my lady's sleepy time, for it is well to make as sure as possible of her gracious smiles by avoiding any infringement on her nap. She may be only six weeks old, and is like a pink rosebud as the nurse carries her about for the company's admiration after the ceremony. She is dressed in the finest and softest gown that can be afforded, all the better if it has been handed down from other family christenings; two rosettes of baby ribbon, white, of course, on the shoulders show that it is "full dress" for her tiny ladyship; and custom likes a small posy of white blossoms tucked in somewhere about her.

She is carried away before long, and refreshments are served, perhaps the traditional caudle, a hot drink made of spiced and sweetened oatmeal water, but the equally old dish formerly concocted for the father and his men friends no longer appears, a fact which no one need regret. This was a mixture of sweetened, buttered toast, with boiling beer poured over; and for each piece of toast a man took from the big bowl, he put in a piece of money for the baby's nurse.

The simplest, and to many people the most refined form of refreshment, is a good wine passed with cake in the parlor. But perhaps the most general thing nowadays is a luncheon, at which the decorations and the dishes should be white as far as possible.

Children's Parties

Miss Baby thus makes her first bow at an early age, but for the next years she keeps to her nursery, growing in sweetness and beauty all the time, until her days of children's parties come. The invitations for these give room for any amount of prettiness and ingenuity. They may be written by the mother, or the child may pen them in his or her own wabbly characters; they may be in rhyme, or may be decorated with tiny water colors of Mother Goose people, or any other suitable subject. The little guests all reply as soon as possible, having also a wide range in the matter of their notes.

There are a few secrets about making a party for little folks successful. There should be as much music as possible; the games should be well planned beforehand, so that no drags occur; the refreshments must be simple and wholesome, and easily handled by chubby fingers; and instead of one or two handsome prizes for skill in certain games, the aim should be to see that every child carries home some pretty trifle in the way of a favor. If the occasion is a birthday, and the guests bring gifts, good taste demands that these be simple and inexpensive; and a wise mother takes this occasion to teach my lady the why of removing cards from presents, explaining that their display invites comparison which is unpleasant.

Indeed the value of these little parties as an opportunity to inculcate the principles of good breeding is very great; for the man or woman who learns manners and deportment before the age of ten never loses them in the sixty or more years of after life.

My lady and her brothers will go to children's parties until well on in their teens, when gradually they find themselves siding off into informal-clubs and societies at church and at school. The girls meet together from house to house, either to sew dainty things for charity, or to twang their mandolins and guitars; and the girl hostess has her first experiences with the chafing-dish and ice cream freezer. Occasionally they entertain their brothers; and though the thanks are apt to take the form of teasing and making fun, everybody knows the boys enjoy the feasts, else why do they take the girls coasting, or coax their mothers for little dances and Saturday matinee parties?

Coming-Out Parties

All this time my lady may have her visiting card if she likes, bearing her full name, Elizabeth Martin Graham, either with or without the prefix Miss, and never using a pet name or diminutive. When she is to be introduced into society her name is engraved on her mother's card, thus:

Mrs. Alfred Rogers Graham

Miss Graham

and according to strict convention she must call with

her mother altogether, and wait a year before she can have cards of her own again (using her schoolgirl ones for very informal affairs), after which the bits of pasteboard will be engraved Miss Graham.

The introduction is made at a tea or reception given by the girl's mother; and engraved invitations announcing that Mrs. Alfred Rogers Graham (with Miss Graham's name underneath) will be at home on such a day from 4 until 7, are sent to every lady and gentleman, irrespective of age, with whom the mother desires to keep up her social relations. It is an unforgivable slight to be left out of the number invited to meet one's friend's daughter.

The invitations require no acknowledgment, but flowers may be sent to the girl; and the debutante of to-day has little enough pleasure in this first reception beyond the flowers she receives; for whereas her mother, some twenty odd years ago, was introduced by a grand ball, and danced the night away without a touch of responsibility, my lady is simply and girlishly dressed, with high neck and long sleeves, and spends the time soberly standing at the door by her mother's side, to receive the guests as they come. One of the points a well-bred woman makes on this occasion is to present the girl to the guests, and not the guests to the debutante.

The visitors speak with their hostesses a minute or two and then greet other friends; and it may be remarked here that even in the most informal call a man or woman of good manners always speaks to the hostess before recognizing anyone else who may be present. It is a mark of ill-breeding among the guests if the mother and daughter are left standing alone at the door; but when others crowd about them you may pass on into the room where refreshments are being served, and may finally slip away without good-byes. Even this apparent rudeness has its reason in a nicety of feeling, and the present-day function is all the pleasanter for not being broken up by the alarm of the first retiring guest's expression of thanks.

My lady is now grown up, and is invited to all the entertainments given by her mother's friends; and of course she knows that to get pleasure from social intercourse with men and women she must be dominated by the social feeling—the desire and determination to be happy in things as they come, rather than to set her heart in certain directions and strive to bend the world that way. She is, therefore, sweet-tempered and smiling on all occasions, witty only when her sharpness is complimentary, with eyes and ears and heart open to other people's charms, and deaf and blind to those unpleasantnesses which are sure to occur in her presence from time to time.

LUNCHEONS, DINNERS AND WEDDINGS

Luncheons and Breakfasts

After nibbling at all the gayeties in turn, my lady finds that nothing is more real pleasure than a luncheon.

It may be a formal affair in honor of some visiting lady —men and luncheons rarely go together—or just a small gathering of friends to chat over a dainty dish for which the hostess is famed in her admiring circle. In either case wines are going out of style, and effervescent waters are more and more used in their place. All one's artistic taste may be used in decorating the luncheon table, as it belongs more individually to the hostess than that for the soberer dinner; and though fashion declares favors out of grace just now, it is no offense against good form to have at each place some trifle which by its pleasant humor will add to the merriment of the party.

In fact, conventionality has never got a good grip on the luncheon; and though engraved cards are sometimes used and elaborate courses follow each other on the dainty table, nobody wants to be stiff, and any agreeable innovation on the part of the hostess is sure to be appreciated.

When luncheon is announced the hostess leads the way to the dining room without formality, and seats her guests, and if she is wise she has thought out the matter of congenial neighbors with as much care as for a dinner; or she may find place cards convenient, and they are entirely correct.

The hour for luncheon is usually half after 1, the matter of time being its chief distinction from a breakfast, as the latter is served at noon; though another point of difference is that while luncheons are frequently given without any more particular meaning than the enjoyment, breakfasts come after certain ceremonies or occasions, as for instance, a wedding breakfast or a hunt breakfast.

Formal Dinners

Dinners are the weightiest of all entertainment, from every point of view, and despite the present movement toward simplicity of food, the courses remain as many and as elaborate as the hostess dares undertake, but she must surely not dare more than she can carry through.

People who give many dinners keep on hand engraved invitation cards, into which the name and date are written. These are sent out about two weeks in advance, or earlier if the guest is apt to be very much engaged. Every member of the household who is to be present at the table should be in the drawing room to greet the arriving guests; and guests should avoid with equal care a too early and a tardy arrival. The dinner hour varies from half after 6 to 8 o'clock.

The formal practice of having a servant present to each man guest a salver from which he takes an envelope addressed to himself containing on the card the name of his partner for dinner, is obviated at most home dinners by more original and often entertaining devices. The host with the chief lady guest passes to the farther end of the dining room, the other couples follow more or less formally, the hostess coming last with the man she wishes to honor.

It is quite within the bounds of good taste for the table to be lavish with silver, fine linen and flowers, but there must be no useless pieces; everything must fill a need, and the *tout ensemble* must have the appearance of being planned for the convenience and delight of the guests and not for vulgar display of wealth. The lighting must be so arranged as to throw nobody into a disagreeable or unbecoming shadow, and the decorations should not be high enough to obstruct the view between any two persons.

The forks are used as they come, beginning with the outermost one. If one wishes to decline wine, it is done by a quiet word or gesture to the servant.

It is correct in these sensible times to enjoy the goodly feast set before you, keeping your enjoyment within bounds, and doing your part toward the dinner talk.

The hostess gives the sign to rise and the men stand until the ladies have passed out, then return to the table for wine and cigars, while coffee is served in the drawing room. If one woman is specially honored by the dinner, she is the first to leave, about an hour after the men have returned to the drawing room; and it need hardly be mentioned that any entertainment where one has been feasted in a particularly reserved seat and one of an exclusively chosen party demands good-byes and a pleasant word of appreciation to the hostess. No slipping away after a dinner, luncheon or breakfast.

Weddings

One morning in May after my lady has been out some two years, the postman leaves at the door of a certain house a large thick white envelope, sealed and bearing a two-cent stamp. Mrs. Bennett opens it at the tete-a-tete breakfast and hands it to her husband, with the comment that she knew it could not be put off much longer, Bess was too pretty, and Mr. Bennett reads in Old English engraved letters:

> Dr. and Mrs. Alfred Rogers Graham
> request the honor of
> Mr. and Mrs. Bennett's
> presence at the marriage of their daughter
> Elizabeth Martin
> and
> Mr. Thomas Mason
> on Wednesday, June the eighth
> at twelve o'clock
> Grace Church

"May weddings are unlucky," his wife adds, "I am glad they put it well into June."

Presents begin to pour into the Graham house, and my lady, being trained in gentle manners from her babyhood, arranges them to be looked at; and when she takes off the cards makes a note on each one of just which gift it accompanied, lest she forget before she is well accustomed to the many new possessions. In her note of thanks to each friend she mentions the article specifically, thus showing that she is not careless of it nor of the giver.

All the shopping and sewing is finished a week before the wedding day, and my lady devotes the time, the prospective groom being considerate on this point, to her parents and brothers. She has many things to arrange, however; she asks certain girl friends to be her attendants, the dearest of all the maid (sometimes matron) of honor, and plans with them their gowns, remembering to select fabric and style suitable for other occasions later on, in case the girls be not well-to-do.

After the wedding there is a reception at the home of the bride's parents, and so quietly have the plans been laid that while the guests are enjoying the luncheon at the small tables scattered through three rooms, somebody laughingly calls out that the young couple is stealing into a carriage to slip off to the train. Then there is a merry scramble to the front door, and the traditional rice and old shoes are thrown after the already speeding carriage. The shoe custom has its meaning, so says one authority at least, in the idea that the young husband with such a weapon may enforce the obedience promised at the altar. The honeymoon is spent at the country house of some friend, or on a houseboat, and after the four weeks a little trip across the waters is much favored in the smart set.

Shortly after the wedding a call is due the bride's mother from each one who received an invitation, and the bride must also be called on as soon as she has returned and is settled down.

The next years bring a continuation of the gayeties of young ladyhood. It is not strictly good form for a young matron to chaperon girls no younger or less experienced than herself; neither she nor her husband may be invited alone to any function where both men and women are to be present, nor may one accept an invitation which the other declines, unless there is some unusual and very good reason, in which case the wife would go with her mother, or chaperoned like an unmarried woman.

In Bereavement

As life goes on, sorrows as well as joys come to my lady. Mr. Bennett, a family friend, dies, and flowers are sent to the house, no longer great set forms, nor exclusively white and purple blossoms, but long-stemmed flowers of any color, tied with white satin ribbons. My lady calls on Mrs. Bennett, and though she does not see her, leaves a note expressing in a few simple words her affection and sympathy. The only possible comfort one can give in time of bereavement is the assurance that the sorrow is shared by all the circle of friends. It is not the time for a sermon but for words of human love. Where the number of letters of condolence is too large to be answered with personal notes, it is sometimes the custom of the mourning family to issue small black-bordered cards, engraved with a few lines of appreciation.

Wedding Anniversaries

The first wedding anniversaries are celebrated with merrymakings of any kind that may be suitable. Friends shower the couple with tin, wooden and glass things in their proper turn; but when the silver wedding comes around everybody is apt to have grown soberer. There is less frolicking, and more serious rejoicing; and as silver is of greater value than tin and wood, it is good form only for relatives and close friends to make gifts at this celebration.

Happy is my lady in having her mother still beside her at the silver wedding; and when fifty years have passed since that June marriage day, and the golden wedding cards go out to the narrowing circle of old-time friends, thrice blessed is she because of the sons and daughters to the third generation gathered about her chair. The cards are engraved in gold, and bear the names of the one-time boy and girl, with the date of their marriage, above the invitation to the reception. In the lower left corner appear the words No presents; for indeed my lady feels that she has had her share of the material things of earth, and that nothing can add one jot to the joy of seeing about her the faces of those she loves. She smiles serenely at the great cup her sons and grandsons bring to the white-haired lovers; and says, as she strokes the head of the boy at her knee: "It is beautiful, but it is not purer gold than I have had in my life since I saw the curls of my first baby— your grandmother, my dear."

And thus we may well leave her; caressing the soft golden hair of the youngest of her blood, her other hand clasped in that one which has led her tenderly and well from a blossoming maidenhood into the perfect flower of a gracious and beauteous old age.

DINNERS

DINNERS

A DAINTY JUNE DINNER

By Anne Warner

"And little recks to find the way to heaven
By doing deeds of hospitality."—Shakespeare.

COMMON sense and a little experience soon enable one who so wills it to be an easy, if unpretentious, dispenser of many forms of entertainment in a home—to become "given to hospitality." A dinner, however, should have something of a ceremonious character; the name carries with it certain obligations and dignities. The true gourmet insists that at this meal, at least, the napery, the lights, the service, the materials and the cooking of them shall be the best to be obtained, circumstances considered, for the gourmet is also a philosopher. A wise woman always endeavors to suit her menu to the season, and it is easy indeed to tempt the early summer appetite. Moderation is the golden rule of dinner giving, and quality, not quantity, is what pleases; overcrowding dishes is a mistake common to beginners, yet variety we all desire. With cold storage, quick transportation, kiln drying, modern canning and the hothouse, almost every delicacy may be had the year round—if the purse is long—but fortunately this condition of things does not take the keen edge of delight from the first native-grown asparagus or strawberries or early peas, home garden tomatoes or new potatoes. All through the spring, one good thing swiftly follows another, and the peculiar pleasure one has in fish, flesh and vegetables comes from their absolute freshness. It seems to me that the labor of making sure that supplies are fresh is effort well expended.

While upholding the dignity of the dinner table, I also believe in a degree of independence concerning certain accepted rules, latitude enough to allow every guest and every "peculiar" member of the family to enjoy himself to the full. I have lately read that "a hostess should never risk her reputation by serving butter at dinner"—and I still serve it! When tempted to leave off the butter plates I remember a certain holiday long ago when we were all bidden to a neighbor's to dine. The children sat at a separate table, as small boys abounded in both families. Butter not being forthcoming, my youngest brother, after a brief consultation with the next older, left the festive board, ran home and returned with a pound roll of the desired lubricant, which his favored table proceeded to enjoy in all sobriety and innocence. I have often seen men at butterless dinners whom I know would have gladly run a mile to supply the deficiency, so why, in all conscience, not offer butter to take or leave? For those to whom it seems as out of place at dinner as pie at breakfast—a gastronomic crime—it is well to instruct the cook to roll the biscuit dough very thin; cut it into strips and roll these on the board till even and well rounded; brush with softened butter and braid or **twist. Cut into** finger-lengths and pinch the ends together. The pocket-book shape makes an excellent dinner roll because of the generous piece of butter which can be put between the "flaps" before raising.

For the following dinner the table, covered with a fine cloth, was adorned further with a Benares brass tray twelve inches square, the center containing a circular mound of wet moss filled with beautiful pansy blossoms of all colors. The tray was set cornerwise on a round centerpiece richly embroidered in yellow. Four antique brass candlesticks, holding candles with large fluffy yellow silk shades, stood at equal distances about the centerpiece. Above the table was suspended a bell-shaped piece of perforated brass—rescued from a curio shop—fitted with electric bulbs and having a deep fringe of tiny gilt-lined glass beads. This arrangement cast a soft and pleasant light, upon which the success of all decoration so largely depends. Beside each plate was placed a small Benares tray holding a tall straight glass ornamented in gold. At the fourth course the glasses were half filled with shaved ice, and a maple punch made from an old and much prized family recipe was served in them. The proportions for this are one glass of water, one glass of Jamaica rum, three-quarters glass of strained lemon juice and one-half glass of maple syrup. Bottle and keep on ice. In serving dilute to taste with table or iced water. The small dishes on the table were odd pieces of brass, lined with a lettuce leaf, a dainty bit of lace work or a glass saucer, as the case called for. This decorative scheme was used later for a luncheon, and most effective it proved to be on a bare table. Scattered pansies took the place of the candlesticks, one of my "notions" being never—with malice aforethought—to use artificial light when I can have God's sunshine. In the luncheon menu a suitable course was substituted for the roast and the bouillon was replaced by French strawberries, as the day was warm.

French Strawberries—Fill punch cups one-third full of very ripe red berries, sliced; add a tablespoon of granulated sugar to each cup and fill three-quarters full with strained orange juice. Stir gently to dissolve sugar and set the cups into a pan of cracked ice till served. When these simple ingredients are first put together the combination of color is really dreadful to contemplate, so give the mixture at least three hours to ripen and beautify. Valencia oranges are the most satisfactory for this use at this time of year.

MENU

Chicken bouillon   Soup balls

Pulled bread

Soft shell crabs   Sauce tartare   Rolls

Scotch eggs   Olives   Bechamel sauce

Sirloin roast

Potato puff   Savory carrots

Spring salad   Cheese (in good company)

Angel parfait   Marrons in coffee sauce

Sponge cake

Salted pecans   Black coffee

There is a chicken bouillon prepared for invalids, which comes in half-pint cans. It is better than any I have been able to make for well people. Heat it and add just before serving the

Soup Balls—Chop the white meat of a chicken very fine and season highly with salt, pepper, onion juice and a little thyme or curry; add enough yolk of egg to bind together. Roll into very small balls, shake in a plate of flour till covered and poach in boiling water. You will find the pulled bread in its perfection at the baker's.

Have the crabs dressed at the market, but look them over carefully and wash before cooking. Dry them well, season with salt and pepper, dredge with flour and saute on both sides. Serve on a hot platter garnished with lemon, and pass

Sauce Tartare—Stir into a cup of mayonnaise, two small sweet-pickled cucumbers, three olives and a handful of watercress chopped fine; a few capers and a little onion juice.

If you live in that happy valley where you can get a *fresh* shad for this course, by all means substitute it. Broil it, garnish with quarters of lemon and with the roe, parboiled and boiled brown; rub with butter frequently while over the fire. Many like shad spread with maitre d'hotel butter—the best of butter, lemon and chopped parsley mixed. To many more this fish is synonymous with bones, their natural inheritance; but let us eat them as they are with thankful hearts, hoping for the day when the scientists will present us with boneless shad as they have with seedless oranges. It has been demonstrated that shad can be boned, with patience, practice, know how and a small sharp knife; the writer has yet to see a shad boned that is not a fish spoiled.

Scotch Eggs—Cook six eggs hard and at the same time keep them tender by leaving in hot water just below the boiling point for one-half hour; cool and remove the shells. Cook to a paste one-third of a cupful of bread crumbs in one-third of a cupful of milk and add one cupful of deviled ham and one raw egg. Cover the eggs with the mixture, roll in crumbs and fry brown in hot fat. Cut in halves lengthwise and send to table on a bed of parsley and garnish with bacon cooked in the manner given below: Slice as thin as possible. Hold the bacon, rind down, and do not try to cut through it till you have the required number of slices, then shave it all at one time from the rind. Separate the slices and lay on a fine wire broiler, put over a pan and place in a hot oven till the bacon is transparent.

Your "John Anderson" may dote on carving; he may have respect for the symmetry of your table appointments; he may be grace and skill combined and personified; if so, I have no suggestions to offer anent the serving of a roast. We have it carved, at the latest possible moment, and set before the host to be distributed with pleasure to all, more especially perhaps to the host and his opposite. The necessary cutting can be done in the kitchen without greatly changing the appearance of the dish.

Potato Puff—Soak old potatoes for several hours and boil in salted water. To two cups of potato mashed or put through a ricer add two tablespoons of butter, one teaspoon of salt and a little white pepper; fold in the whites of two eggs whipped stiff. Bake in a buttered dish. Or dare to serve that almost unheard-of dainty, plain, well-boiled potatoes—Bermudas—and send round a gravy made in the old-fashioned way in the roasting pan. Is there anything much better?

Savory Carrots—Scrape, then cut new carrots into straws. Cook tender in salted water and drain dry. Season with salt, pepper and a little onion juice and return to the kettle with a generous piece of butter and shake till hot and glazed. Pile on a dish in pyramid form, add a cup of fresh green peas well seasoned and a sprinkling of chopped parsley.

Simple and apparently very acceptable individual salads of lettuce hearts, sprinkled with celery seed and glazed with French dressing, came next. Roquefort cheese in a dish with a cover was passed at the same time "for them as wanted it"; also cream cheese and white bar-le-duc, with toasted wafers and unsalted butter, a delightful combination.

Angel Parfait (M Ronald)—Whip whites of three eggs to a stiff froth. Put half a cupful of sugar and same of water into a saucepan on the fire. Stir until the sugar is dissolved, then cook slowly, without touching, till a little dropped into cold water will form a ball when rolled between the fingers. Pour three tablespoonfuls of the boiling hot syrup slowly onto the whipped whites, beating constantly. Add a teaspoonful of noyan, and when cold, a pint of cream, whipped stiff. Mold and pack in a form (with a flat top) for four hours. Vanilla mousse can be used as the base of the dessert, if preferred.

Marrons in Coffee Sauce—Heat in a saucepan one-half a cupful of black coffee and one-quarter cupful of thick cream; thicken with the yolks of two eggs and two teaspoons of sugar beaten together. Drain brandied marrons, cut in halves if very large, and add to the sauce while hot, but set away to get cold before either pouring over the parfait or passing with it. Eat with fresh homemade sponge cake. I experimented with a bottle of noisettes in marasquin as a sauce for a parfait with great success not long ago, but at this season the use of all such fol-de-rols presupposes that you have had strawberries for breakfast and luncheon, and crave "the spice of life."

AN ABBREVIATED DINNER

By Bee Practical

Whether the majority of people have wearied of "china dinners" or simply crave change, the dinner of a few courses is certainly "in." A roast is looked upon as an intrusion; even the sweet is getting lighter, and moderation reigns. The funny man says that present methods in cookery have brought it about that many would rather cook than eat—by making it more fun

to cook and less fun to eat! I hope his wife will invite
him and a few of his cronies to try the following menu:

Tomatoes en surprise
Fillets of flounder stuffed
Savory crusts

Cucumbers	Potatoes
Duck	Orange smack
Olives	Rolls
Turquoise salad	Toasted wafers

Baked Alaskas
Crystallized pineapple and ginger
Orange curacoa

This was recently served at a table with unique
decorations. A large globe of Japanese goldfish rested
on a circular mirror mat, the latter surrounded by a
full border of maidenhair fern. By the way, keep this
fern either submerged, or well sprinkled with water,
and in a cool place, till the last possible moment, before
arranging. Abnormal in form and beautiful in color
were some of the strange little water jewels; rare
mother-of-pearl fringe-tails, bright gold lace and fan-
tails, comets and shining black telescopes. The flashes
from their continuous motion made a centerpiece which
vied in brilliancy and oriental effect with the candle
shades of iridescent beads which ornamented the candles
at the corners of the table. The shades were strung of
beads of different colors and sizes and had a fringe of
the same. Fastened on to wire frames they well repay
the trouble of making, as they are not perishable.

At each place was a small green jardiniere holding a pot of growing ferns, queer and unusual varieties being selected. Upright in the foliage appeared a miniature bamboo rod with a line attached, from which dangled a realistic goldfish (caught at the caterer's) and made to do duty as a name card. Just before the finger bowls were set on, two or three magic flowers were dropped into each. These blossom "while you wait" and can be purchased at any Japanese store.

For the first dish, if you will go yourself to a hot-house for the tomatoes, you may be able to get them with the pretty green calyx left on each, to make a handle to the slice you cut from the stem end for a cover. Otherwise insert a large clove, or an apple stem, or even a wooden toothpick wound with ribbon, to serve the purpose. Peel the tomatoes and ice them after taking out the seeds. Mix the pulp with small, choice oysters or clams, season with equal parts of chili sauce and catsup, and add horse-radish, paprika and lemon juice to taste. Fill the tomatoes, put on the covers and serve in glass sauce dishes containing shaved ice. Eat cup and all.

Have the fillets cut from small fish; they are more delicate. Wash, dry, roll in seasoned flour and put a layer in a buttered roasting pan. Make a stuffing by mixing thoroughly half a tablespoon of flour, two of butter, yolks of two eggs, a teaspoon of salt, saltspoon of white pepper and a dash of red, and the following herbs chopped very fine: one teaspoon each of onions and parsley, two tablespoons of celery and a quarter of a can of French mushrooms. Spread a layer over each fillet and cover with another fillet. Protect with a buttered paper and bake in a hot oven twelve or fifteen minutes. Remove the paper, drain the remaining mushrooms, add them to the fish and cook three minutes more. Serve very hot and squeeze over them a quarter of a lemon and arrange the buttons around.

Cut the tops from small rolls and remove the soft inside, for the crusts; butter and brown in the oven. Make a rich white sauce, using asparagus liquor and cream for wetting. Add two cups of asparagus tips and one of peas, and fill the shells.

Prepare the cucumbers as usual; dry and season with a dressing made the same as French dressing, substituting thick cream in place of oil (a new wrinkle), and sprinkle the whole with chopped chives. Let the potatoes be of the Saratoga order, though the accommodating tuber may be contorted and convoluted by novelty cutters, or beguiled into any admired shape.

Serve half a duck breast to a person, and have enough for a second helping. When partly roasted, baste with a little Madeira and cook until the blood is out, but not the juice. There are some who profess to like their duck "run through the oven," but they are the minority. The side dish with this course is made by slicing sour oranges and sprinkling them with a mixture of Maraschino, brandy and orange bitters. Apple sauce, in quarters or sifted—hot or cold—is always acceptable with duck, and olive sauce is relished by many.

The turquoise salad—so it is called at a world-renowned hostelry—was evidently named by the rule of contraries. We rechristened it coral salad. The ingredients are shredded celery, bleached romaine and pimentoes cut in long, slender pieces; the proportion of celery being somewhat greater than the other two. Romaine is not always to be had, but lettuce is ever with us. The dressing is mayonnaise and—between us—the best hotel dressing never equals the homemade product. Each plate holds an added tidbit made of a crisp, tender stalk of celery selected from those growing just outside the heart. The concave side of the stalk is heaped with cream cheese, seasoned, moistened with a little cream or dressing, and mixed with chopped walnut meats. This novel garnish is eaten from the fingers as if the celery were plain, and the whole combination is most delicious—if the inventor *was* color blind! A touch of red can be put in the cheese if desired.

Of the tantalizing sort is the dessert, the kind that makes one resolve to find opportunity to try her hand at it without delay. Yet it is, perhaps, too difficult for an amateur to undertake. Fill small pyramid molds with French ice cream. Always a solid, fine-grained cream, for this purpose it should have been made still more solid by an additional number of egg yolks. Put the molds into a freezing box or into a pail. Seal the joints of the pail tightly with butter and bury in ice and salt. Molds packed in this way require to stand longer than those which come in direct contact with the freezing mixture, and these *must* be veritable

Alaskas for coldness. Prepare discs of sponge cake the size of the flat surface of the molds and three-quarters of an inch thick, and set at some distance apart on a hardwood board covered with waxed paper. Make a meringue, allowing one-quarter cup of powdered sugar and a sprinkle of salt to each egg white; beat till smooth and firm enough to hold its shape. Unmold the cones of cream with great care, set the base of each on to a circle of cake, coat *instanter* with a covering of meringue and color slightly on the top slide of a piping hot open; or, far better, brown separately and evenly with a salamander iron. The Alaskas are usually large enough to cut in halves at the table, making two portions.

Savarin said: "The discovery of a new dish does more for the happiness of the human race than the discovery of a planet." But if there are "nerves" in the kitchen, either when you are there or not, serve the following older delicacy: Line a melon mold with a thin layer of pistachio ice cream; nearly fill the center with French cream (which is yellow), leaving a small space in the center of this to be filled with pignolias mixed with barely enough cream to bind them together. Repack in ice and salt to ripen. Thickly strew the surface of the melon when unmolded with the same nuts—or almonds—browned and chopped, to simulate a rind. Trim plate with maidenhair.

For orange curacoa, thoroughly clean the rind, then make cups of tough-skinned oranges by cutting in halves crosswise and turning the peel backward. Set pulp side down on a small plate containing a coffee spoon, and serve one to each individual. Said individuals help themselves to a lump or two of loaf sugar and a tablespoon of brandy, when these are passed, and the host then starts a tiny alcohol lamp and matches round the table to light the brew. A little manipulation with the spoon extracts the essential oil from the peel while the liquor is burning away, and a seasoning of mace and cinnamon may be added during this process if it is considered an improvement. The remaining liquid is sipped from the spoon when the flame has subsided; if preferred, it may be poured into a cordial glass of fine ice, or be added to the black coffee. Some cherish the illusion that this is the Olympian nectar, and others—hold a different opinion; but whichever view one takes, 'tis an excellent digester and a very pretty after-dinner plaything.

A COMPANY DINNER

By Anne Warner

Menu cards are no longer used on private tables. Place cards, either perfectly plain or beautifully decorated for souvenirs, each bearing the name of a guest, may be put at the side of the plates. They are useful in indicating the seat which each member of the party is to occupy. If wine or mineral water is to be served and a cooler is not at hand, put the bottles in a pail with crushed ice and a little rock salt, and cover with a piece of carpet. Submerge the body of the bottles only. This precaution will do away with the necessity of rinsing the salt water from about the corks, sometimes a difficult task. It is well to have a doily wrapped round the bottle for convenience in serving, unless the host objects when it covers a label dated B. C.

On this dinner ' table two Dresden candelabra, holding groups of candles with semi-transparent painted shades, stood together, high in the center. The table was covered with a mass of pink June roses mixed with foliage, leaving only enough space around the edge to hold plates, glasses and other necessaries. The roses shaded from dark pink ones in the center to pale pink at the edge, and the arrangement caused much enthusiasm (and a great dearth in the garden). The stems were cut short and stuck into wet sand in flat tins, which held them firmly in place and kept them fresh. The light of the room was concentrated upon the table, making it the center of attraction, as it should be. The dessert plates and after-dinner coffee cups were Dresden china.

MENU

Clams   Radishes   Sandwiches

Consomme royale   Olives   Wafers

Brook trout   Cresses   Rolls

Saddle of lamb   Mint sauce

Asparagus   Potato apples

Currant jelly   Strawberry punch

Summer salad   Cheese balls

Sandwiches
Prune souffle   Brandy sauce
Figs in cordial   Salted almonds
Black coffee

Serve the clams on the shells in deep plates of cracked ice, with a radish in the center of each dish. Leave a bit of the green stem, cut and turn back five strips of the red peel of the radishes. Mix a little horse-radish with butter for the filling of the sandwiches and cut in any pretty shape.

The consomme should be clarified till brilliant. For the custard beat two eggs moderately, add two tablespoonfuls of milk and season with pepper and salt. Butter a large flat pan, set it in another one containing hot water and bake very slowly till set. It should not even brown on top. When the soup is in the tureen, cut the custards into forms with a tiny fancy cutter, without first removing from the pan, and add carefully to the consomme.

If the annual trouting fever "strikes" one of your family, then is the time to give this dinner; but if the attack comes inconveniently, do the next best thing. What you want is fresh brook trout. Almost all hotels and some markets have chances to buy these of "lone fishermen," and will do you the favor (and it *is* a favor) of getting them for you. When the trout are dressed, dry thoroughly with a soft cloth and sprinkle inside with a little pepper (that is what my fisherman says!). Roll in Indian meal and saute in hot salt pork fat.

Serve in a border of watercresses and do not spoil with
other relishes or sauces.

Have the saddle well done and carved in long thin
slices parallel with the bone, if the lamb is heavy, or
across and serve the ribs if very small. Use the tender
tips of mint only, for the sauce. Stand for an hour
or so in about half a cup of mild vinegar mixed with
two tablespoonfuls of sugar. Wash the asparagus carefully and tie into bundles. Cut from the tough end
of the stalks enough to make them of uniform length
and boil in salted water till tender, but not limp. Put
on buttered toast, cut and pull off the strings and
season with salt and pepper and melted butter. Use
an asparagus fork for serving.

Prune Souffle—Wash one-half pound of sweet
prunes; soak over night, cook soft, remove the stones
and chop *fine*. Whip the whites of four eggs stiff;
gradually adding one-half a cupful of powdered sugar
and a pinch of cream of tartar. Fold lightly into the
prunes and bake about twenty minutes in a buttered
pudding dish. Serve either with whipped cream
sweetened and flavored and the figs in cordial, or with
a foamy brandy sauce. It is better hot. If you have
no holder for the pudding dish it can be made more
presentable by folding a large napkin cornerwise and
pinning (invisibly) around the dish and setting on a
pretty plate.

Potato Apples—Prepare a croquette mixture, form
into small balls and roll in eggs and crumbs. Flatten
slightly and put a clove in one side for the eye; make

a little depression in the opposite side and stick in it an apple stem and fry. By shaping differently you can have "pears," if you like.

Strawberry Punch—Boil a quart of water and two and one-half cupfuls of sugar for about ten minutes, add one cupful and a quarter of strawberry juice, and cool. Before freezing add half a cupful of Maraschino and it will then not freeze hard. Serve in cups.

Summer Salad—Select six fresh cucumbers all the same size. Pare, cut in halves lengthwise, scoop out the centers and lay in water till wanted. Dry and fill with a mixture of sweetbreads and peas, dressed with mayonnaise. Set on a green lettuce leaf on individual plates. Serve with dainty plain bread and butter sandwiches and

Cheese Balls—Mix thoroughly a cup and a half of grated cheese, a little salt and pepper and the whites of three eggs, beaten stiff. Shape into little rolls, cover with bread *dust,* fry in deep fat and drain on blotting paper.

The dessert for this month is strawberries, if you can get them in their perfection; but market strawberries are so seldom anything but a "delusion and a snare!" If you use them, substitute some other fruit juice in the punch. The black coffee may be made over an alcohol lamp, at table, or in a French drip coffee pot; or better still, be served to the guests after they have left the dining room.

THE HARVEST HOME

By Anne Warner

That is what we call it—this dinner that ends our autumn holiday. The garnerings of the outing are pure air, fresh odors and pleasant sights, relaxed nerves, sweetened tempers, rested bodies—and appetites. The capsheaf is the harvest home. The one described here is one of a number that have been enjoyed by a fortunate few at the termination of extended annual drives through the Berkshire hills.

It is an unwritten law of the party that the dinner, whether given at the home of the genial host of these pleasure trips, or at the country house of one of his guests, shall be celebrated in the open air; so, out in the indefinable atmosphere of this season, before the dreamy hush of autumn becomes oppressive, while the hazy air contains no dampness and the chill of evening brings nothing but a feeling of exhilaration, the little parting feast of good things is spread. That is to say, *sometimes*—but tell it not to a native of New England without this word of reservation. Truly our perfect October day is bright and beautiful as a rainbow, but alas, as brief and fugitive; therefore, the stay-at-home, combining a knowledge of this fact with that of the unreliability of men and horses, served this particular dinner on the large hospitable veranda—thus keeping within the letter of the law—and was justified when the wayfarers appeared two hours later than schedule time, with an early hunter's moon sulking behind a cloud.

Across the one end of the veranda where possibly the outside world might peep in, she put a close row of small evergreen trees, making an effective screen and background; while, arranged in corners, enveloping pillars, hanging from every available cornice and ornament, "October's crimson banners flew." A flaming maple, whose changing foliage had been watched for days, contributed largely, and with long branches of richly-tinted, shining oak leaves and a touch of the yellow and brown of chestnut leaves and burs, combined to make a place beautiful to the eye; while hidden among these, bunches of wild grapes still on the vines, added their ineffable but unmistakable incense, to the gratification of another sense.

The center of the table held a large loosely-woven grass basket, tipped on its side and pouring forth evidence of the maturity and bounty of the "fall o' the year." Clusters of purple Concord grapes, golden-green Niagaras and tiny pink Delawares blended their bloom and color in the profusion that tumbled out among the soft tufts of a tangle of feathery clematis vine, which started under the basket and ran with riotous and apparently unstudied freedom over the cloth. Nothing of a hothouse growth may come to these feasts, if you please—consistency, thou art a jewel!

The place cards were rolls of thin birch bark which curled round the extreme ends of the clematis. When "night threw her mantle o'er the skies and pinned it

with a star," the table was lighted by the twinkling
beams from many unshaded bayberry candles. These
candles, by the way, are made by an old resident back
in the country on Long Island and are the result of a
mysterious process of extracting the wax from bay-
berries. They are green in color and give out a faint
odor favorable to reminiscence. And now to the baser
attractions of the menu.

Clams

Corn soup   Croutons

Smelts   Sauce tartare

Tomatoes   Rolls

Saddle venison   Jelly sauce

Sweet potatoes   Brussels sprouts

Boiled chestnuts

Roman punch

Broiled quail   Hominy crescents

October salad

Grandmother's pudding   Snowdrift sauce

Fig dainty

Grapes   Cheese and wafers   Coffee

At each cover the clams radiated from the conventional lemon half, but the latter rested within a little
circle of the choicest of the late flowering nasturtiums
that the garden afforded. The sandwiches served with
them were made of thin buttered rounds of white bread,
with a filling of spicy nasturtium petals and very young
leaves. The condiments were green pepper sauce—
and hunger.

Outspoken members of the family go so far as to say that they know with absolute certainty what soup will invariably be offered during the corn season, if the stay-at-home has control of the menu. It seems so excellent to her that she offers the recipe here.

Corn Soup—One pint of corn pulp, the kernels having been slashed with a sharp knife and the corn *scraped* from the cob. Three pints of boiling water, one of rich milk, one cup of white stock, three tablespoons of butter, one tablespoon of flour; yolks of two eggs, pepper, salt and a few drops of onion juice. Cook the cobs in the water twenty minutes; remove them, add corn pulp and boil the same length of time; rub through a colander—nearly all should pass through if the corn has been properly prepared. Season, cover and keep hot. Make a smooth white sauce of the butter, flour and stock in the regular way; add to the soup and boil up together. Heat the milk in another saucepan, pour upon the beaten yolks and cook one minute; season, stir both parts together, and when in the tureen garnish with whipped cream "stars." Serve with hot buttered croutons. The only drawback to the ordinary use of this soup at dinner is that it is a whole meal in itself; it needs a "touring" appetite.

October is the appointed time to eat green smelts in any case, and to the hill travelers they were doubly acceptable, for, as one of them said: "We haven't had anything in or on the fish line between Cape Cod turkey and trout!"

Fried Smelts—Selected smelts were washed, dried,

sprinkled with salt and pepper, dipped in cream and rolled in very fine bread crumbs. They had been made into rings by gashing diagonally and pinning head and tail together with wooden toothpicks (removed after frying), and were cooked in a wire basket in deep fat. They appeared at table on a round platter covered with a folded napkin, were garnished with parsley, and served with their sauce, tiny rolls, and ripe, meaty, cold tomatoes.

In cooking venison, first and foremost it is to be remembered that it should be rather underdone than otherwise. The finest portion is the saddle; next the haunch, which includes one-half the loin; the third best joint is the neck.

Butter a large sheet of writing paper, sprinkle with salt and place over the fat, make a coarse paste and cover the lean part. Roast in a piping hot oven, basting repeatedly. Fifteen minutes before it is done, remove paper and paste, baste with a little butter, and brown. For sauce, heat together one-half cup of either port or claret and the same of clear stock and pour over a small glass of currant jelly. The chestnuts should be hot and well salted, and have been carefully looked over by the cook before boiling; this should not prevent the partaker from looking them over carefully on his own account.

The methods of preparing the vegetables for this course were specialties of our Southern major-domo.

Sweet Potatoes, Southern Style—In a large, flat-bottomed saucepan melt two heaping tablespoons of butter and one of sugar. Select medium-sized sweet potatoes to pare, cut in two lengthwise and season with salt and pepper. Closely cover the bottom of the kettle with the raw potatoes and put another layer on top. Pour on water to cover the lower layer, cover tightly and place over gentle heat, that the cooking may be slow. When the lower layer is well colored change to the top. By the time both are "dun brown" the water will have evaporated, leaving a very little butter sauce to pour over the potatoes.

Chloe's Brussels Sprouts—Remove any wilted leaves from the outside and let the sprouts stand a few minutes in cold water strongly salted. Cook uncovered till tender, in rapidly boiling water. Drain thoroughly, then place in a saucepan containing a generous lump of butter, a Chili pepper and some celery salt, and toss till lightly browned. Just before serving remove the pepper and add a dash each of kitchen bouquet and fine Madeira.

It is doubtless disheartening for epicures to be forced to learn that the prince of American game birds, the woodcock, is becoming extinct. These long-billed martyrs had a place in the original menu of this dinner, which was given before the edict went forth that "it shall be unlawful to buy, sell, or offer for sale, or have in possession for sale, any woodcock or ruffed grouse, commonly called partridge, whenever or wherever the said birds may have been taken or killed." So far, so good, say I! But between the first of October and the first of December we may still

regale ourselves upon—"enjoy," if we can—the "poor
Bob White" till his turn shall come to be protected.
I would go hungry to desperation before I would eat
one, and be the indirect cause of stilling a single throat
that gives his inspiring call; but one must perforce
give up one's whims and notions to others' appetites,
and this is a menu and not a sermon. To be sure,
I eat other game with relish and avidity—didn't I
just say something about consistency?

Hominy Crescents are excellent to serve under
birds. Put one-half cup of hominy in a double boiler
with one-half cup of white stock; soak fifteen minutes,
add one and a half cups hot milk and cook half an
hour. Then stir in thoroughly one-half teaspoon of salt,
one-quarter teaspoon of paprika, a few drops of onion
juice and yolks of two eggs. Turn one-half an inch
thick into a shallow pan; when cold cut into forms,
crumb, egg and fry.

October Salad—Pare Spitzenberg apples and cut
into cubes; cut up an equal quantity of crisp, tender
celery and the same of hickory nut meats. Mix and
dress with a mayonnaise and serve in polished, red-
cheeked apples which have been hollowed out for the
purpose. Set each impromptu dish on a brilliant
autumn leaf.

Grandmother C.'s pudding recipe comes down from
the time when the taste and try method was in vogue,
and descendants of the originator have ever since been
proud to concoct all sizes of it by her elastic rule,
unhampered by so much as a spoon or a cup. I give

it with perhaps overmuch elaboration since hearing one younger branch of the family remark to another branch, with a pessimistic sniff: "What's the use of giving it to anybody; nobody makes it *right,* outside of the family!"

Buy a stale loaf of bread from the baker—a brick loaf—and since you will not be able to get it more than a day old, keep it till it reaches the advanced age of three days. The night before you expect to serve the pudding proceed as follows: With a sharp knife slice the bread very thin ("so that you can *see* through it," says the pessimist); this is imperative. Put a layer in the bottom of the pudding dish—and thereby hangs another tale. This dish must be a heavy earthenware or stone crock, glazed inside and of a shape which resembles a flower pot, high and narrow; I doubt if the pudding can have the proper appearance or flavor made in any other. Prepare the dish for the bread by greasing generously with butter "about the size of an egg." Add to the first layer a "sprinkling" of sugar, "just a pinch" each of allspice and cinnamon, a "grating" of nutmeg and a "good handful" of imported Malaga raisins seeded and cut in halves. Continue in this order till the pudding mold is full, finishing with a layer of bread. Heat a quantity of fresh, rich milk lukewarm; add a "savor" of salt and enough molasses to color the milk perceptibly, and pour slowly over the bread till by gently pressing the mass you can see the milk. Never stir it. Cover with a plate and leave in a moderately warm place all night.

It will shrink a little, and in the morning, if it seems dry, more prepared milk should be added before baking in an even oven for three or four hours, according to size. Keep it covered with an inverted deep plate for two hours of the time, then replace with a piece of brown paper. The pudding has a tendency to burn and must be carefully watched. Let it stand a few minutes when taken from the oven, with the mold wrapped in a folded cloth which has been wrung out of cold water, then put the serving plate over the top and it will turn out without sticking. It should not be stiff enough to keep the exact shape of the deep mold, but sink to a quivering, sponge-like mound covered with a golden crust. Eat with a hard sauce when hot, and with a hot sauce when cold and equally appetizing. This was a favorite Thanksgiving dessert in "ye olden time," and Grandmother's pudding is well worth experimenting with.

Its accompaniments are the innovations of younger generations. The snowdrift sauce is a variety of, and, we think, an improvement upon, the regulation hard sauce. Make fine lemons into cups by cutting them into halves picket fashion. Remove pulp and shave a bit from the bottom of each half to insure a flat surface. Beat together one-half cup of butter and one cup of powdered sugar until very white and light. The success of the sauce depends upon its long beating. Add one-half teaspoon of vanilla, two tablespoons of brandy and one-half a cup of thick whipped cream, or the whipped white of an egg, if preferred. Cool, heap lightly into the lemon cups (Grandmother always wanted a little nutmeg and lemon zest grated over hers) and serve very cold on small individual plates.

Fig Dainty—Wash two pounds of bag figs and stew gently till tender in a little water, the juice of a lemon and half a cup of port. Cool before serving two on each plate with the sauce.

The ripe Gorgonzola brought up the subject of the relative excellence of Italian cheeses, and a member of the party informed us that the experiment had lately been completed of keeping some Parmesan for one hundred and fifty years and that the cheese was found to be still delicious and "full of life and power"; we unanimously voted him guilty of ambiguity, if nothing worse.

One last toast was drunk to the drive of the coming year, in—we will call it cider, as that is seasonable; with jokes and reminiscences and friendly chaffing the guests left the table to gather round an open fire which had been built in the ingle nook of the veranda, while the masculine contingent smoked a peace on earth cigar; and the dinner became one of the "has beens."

THE WINTER FEAST

By B. P.

In thinking over the dinners I have given or have assisted in giving, one belonging to the latter class always looms in my memory above the others, as being

the most difficult, and, at the same time the most
enjoyable of them all (incongruous combination!) We
were enduring the rigors of a northern "spell of
weather," and this, with the difficulties overcome in the
struggle to seat twenty-eight persons at one table, had
something to do with the impression, and maybe the
fact that the dinner gown arrived with the guests was
another reason for it.

If a body could be planner and designer, personal
purchaser and caterer, chief cook, table supervisor and
decorator, wine expert and general manager, without
being smiling hostess as well, how it would simplify
matters. How blest must be that estate when you can
summon a chef and say: "Francois, we have twenty-
eight dining to-night," and presto, it is done, and
well done! I will come to earth and own that this
is not at all the way we did it. We had plenty of
help (?) to be sure, of the kind that (at times) one
would have been glad to assist in finding the bottom
of the Red sea, or some other equally distant main,
but refrained from so doing because they were a little
more useful dry than wet. Incompetence, thou dost
so prevail!

When the question of decoration was being dis-
cussed in family conclave, the thought of the necessary expanse of table linen caused the hostess to exclaim
dejectedly: "I don't know but we'll have to resort
to ribbon furbelows to help out, if the table does look
like a milliner's window; even that is better than allowing a florist to hold high carnival." Having duly

considered the pros and cons of both the practical and the artistic sides of the question, the final plan made us independent of the wiles of the florist, and was, we thought, guiltless of the sin of overembellishment; we didn't mind the work. The table was partly prepared early in the day. In due time the florist was to bring the centerpiece, consisting of a mass of deep red Liberty roses, arranged upright on eight or ten-inch stems, in damp moss, on a shallow oblong basket or pan, the dimensions of which we knew. A piece of mousseline de soie, fifteen yards long and full width, and of the exact shade of the roses, was adjusted and pinned in place, as follows: starting from the center, the mousseline crossed diagonally the space allotted to the flowers; each half, starting diagonally again at the opposite angle, was draped and manipulated across the table and tied into a large, graceful double bow, and its billowy daintiness pulled up here, or pinned down there, till the effect was good; then each long end started across toward the other side of the table, and the same maneuvers were gone through with; then diagonally the fourth time, and the last bow— smaller—was made near the end of the opposite side of the table. (Dear me—I wonder if I could do it from this description!) It is hardly necessary to add that ample space was left along the sides and at the ends for covers, and that members of the family *happened* to sit where the necessary overlapping of tablecloths took place under two of the big bows, and the huge Japanese plates filled with fruit which occupied

the angles opposite them. At the appointed hour, with
the "set piece" (if Liberty roses can ever be said to
be set, with their dainty heads poised on their slender
stems) came quantities of maidenhair ferns, fragrant
freesia sprays, clusters of English violets and a few
loose roses. Nimble and clever fingers arranged these
flowers gracefully and irregularly in and around the
bows of shimmering red, with exquisite and novel
effect. Neither the florist nor the milliner was unpleas-
antly in evidence, but the hand of madame herself
was manifest. Each bow-knot covered the base of a
candelabrum, whose candles glowed softly through thin
cut-silver shades lined with the mousseline.

The dinner was served from the butler's pantry
on individual plates—the more formal way, but the
more convenient for so large a number of guests.

MENU

Raw oysters   Sandwiches

Creamed halibut in cucumbers   Radishes

Terrapin a la Chamberlin

Pickled mangoes

Fillet of beef   Mushroom sauce

Spinach balls   Potato ensemble

Roman punch

Squabs on toast   Celery   Jelly sauce

Tomato cup salads   Welsh sandwiches

Cream a la Grasse

Bonbons   Fruit

Cheese   Black coffee

Oysters are excellent bivalves to which to apply the theory that the natural is always the best; so serve either on their shells on regular oyster plates, or on deep plates filled with cracked ice. Put a tiny shell containing a teaspoonful of horse-radish in the center, where the hinge ends meet. Make delicately thin sandwiches of Boston brown bread and spread with a mixture of equal parts of finely chopped olives and pimentos or green peppers, blended with a little mayonnaise. Keep fresh by directions given before.

Halibut in Cucumbers—Cook the halibut till tender in court bouillon—to two quarts of water add a few slices each of carrot, onion and celery; two or three cloves and peppercorns; a bit each of mace, bay leaf and parsley, a little salt and lemon juice. Drain, and when cool remove skin and bone and pick the fish apart into fine flakes. Make a rich white sauce in the regular way, adding from a quarter to a half teaspoon of curry powder to every two cups of sauce, according to taste. Pare, cut in halves and parboil in bouillon the required number of cucumbers. Scoop out the inside of each half, fill with the creamed fish, cover with prepared crumbs—one-third cup of butter to every cup of dried bread crumbs—and bake about half an hour or less, till the cucumbers are soft, but not till they lose shape. Serve with a lemon point on each plate.

Baltimore Terrapin—If those who eat this "insect" had to prepare him for his final appearance—terrapin would be more plentiful! Dip a very much alive "diamond-back" into hot water and scald till the skin can be removed from head and feet by rubbing with a cloth; and wash—and wash—and *wash!* Return to the kettle, and when the claws are soft it is boiled sufficiently; it took nearly an hour, if I remember, to do ours. Cool and remove the bottom shell first, then cut off the nails and head and take out *carefully* the gall-sack and sand-bag. Contrary to directions, our fastidious taste impelled us to take out also several other suspicious looking bits of internal machinery, leaving the meaty parts, the eggs (accounted a great luxury by epicures), the liver and all the juice. So much we did the day before the feast. Shortly before it is to be eaten place these choice morsels in a stewpan to heat. Make a sauce of the mash 1 and creamed yolks of eight hard-boiled eggs and two tablespoons of fine butter rubbed to a smooth paste and added to a pint of cream, which has been heated in a double boiler; season with cayenne and salt. To this quantity of sauce add one quart of the prepared terrapin and simmer for ten minutes—longer will do no harm. Just at the moment of serving pour in two tablespoons of fine Madeira. Serve this dish very hot. There are small metal cups which come for the purpose, but since we were not supplied—not having terrapin often—we used ordinary deep plates, heated.

Living in a small city, we had to send far afield for some of our materials. The fillets came from a distant base of supplies and one of them was decidedly "ripe"—but what would you, ye seekers after perfection in an imperfect world? Our fillets were larded, and baked in a very hot oven in the usual way. Half an hour before they were done they were covered with long thin pieces cut from peeled bananas. One piece was served on each thick slice of beef, and a ladle of sauce added at the side.

Spinach Balls—Pound to a paste in a mortar the yolks of two hard-boiled eggs, and rub smooth with the yolk of one raw egg; season with salt, a drop of tabasco and a very little melted butter. Mix with one cup of cold cooked spinach, drained and pressed as dry as possible. Make into small balls, roll in flour and fry in a basket a few at a time. Some of these small-family recipes had to be quadrupled to make enough to go round.

Potato Ensemble—Mash and season well a quantity of boiled white potatoes, and to every quart add the beaten yolks of two eggs and two tablespoons of thick cream. Stir over the fire and form into a shapely ring on a greased tin sheet, or pack in a ring mold that opens; brush over with yolk of egg and bake in a slow oven—it should not be browned. To take to table, carefully slip the potato ring onto a large round entree plate; encircle it with a single row of potato marbles rolled in parsley, and heap the center with sweet potato croquettes. This dish was passed, and the combination of the white and green, yellow and golden brown, was very tempting.

The following proportions were adhered to in making the punch, and it was dubbed the "life-saving station": put in the saucepan over the fire three-quarters of a pound of sugar and three pints of water; boil ten

minutes and cool. Freeze, and when nearly frozen stir
into it quickly the strained juice of four lemons and
two gills of old Jamaica rum.

Be sure that the squabs *are* squabs. Tie into shape
with thin slices of bacon over the breasts and roast about
twenty minutes, basting with butter; serve on buttered
toast, with celery hearts and the simplest form of jelly
sauce, made by pouring over a tumbler of currant jelly
at the last moment, three tablespoons of hot port wine.

Tomato Cups—To one can of tomatoes add one
teaspoon each of salt and sugar, a dusting of paprika,
two cloves, a bit of bay leaf and a slice of onion. Boil
together till the tomato is soft, then add three-quarters
of a box of gelatine which has been soaked in one-half
a cup of water. Stir till gelatine is dissolved and strain
twice or till nearly clear. Pour into ice cold crockery
cups (flaring, round-bottomed ones are prettiest) to the
depth of half an inch, and leave till the jelly will barely
support light-weight inner molds, about half an inch
smaller, containing a lump of ice. Aluminum ones are
best, but we managed with tin ones—though we "ought
to not"—by taking them out as soon as the jelly was
firmly set. If the first gelatine is allowed to get too
hard before filling the remaining space between the
molds, the cups will separate at this line when turned
out. Make the cups a day or so before using and keep
in a cold place. Unmold when they are wanted by
filling the inner mold with warm water and lifting out.
Dip the outer china forms into hot water and turn out
the tomato cups. Set each one upon crisp lettuce leaves

which have had a bath of French dressing; fill with
a mixture of two-thirds finely cut celery and one-third
coarsely-chopped English walnuts and broken hickory
nut meats.   Combine these ingredients with a generous
quantity of mayonnaise, and   nish each salad with a
cup of mayonnaise cream dressing, put on with a star
tube, and drop a turned olive into each, if you like.

The salad sandwiches should be long and narrow;
make of white bread and fill with tender, selected watercress, which has been dipped in salted tarragon vinegar,
then shaken dry.

The snowy cream (invariably Philadelphia, when
B. P. is at the helm) had a distinctive taste which
delighted and mystified the somewhat jaded appetite.
It was simply flavored highly with Fleur d'Orange, this
comes from Grasse—one does not have to go there for
it!   Serve from the freezer on small, choice plates and
scatter a teaspoon of freshly grated cocoanut on top
of each mound.

> "An't please your Honor," quoth the Peasant,
> "This same dessert is very pleasant."

The fruit was served by the obliging relatives who
sat nearest, by the aid of grape scissors and a willing
spirit, to all who wished it; cheese and wafers solaced
the others, for to many, "a last course at dinner, wanting
cheese, is like a pretty woman with only one eye."

Leaving men and cigars behind, the hostess led the
ladies to the parlors, where clear black coffee was passed,
followed by creme de menthe in glasses filled with

shaved ice, the gentlemen being served in the dining room at the same time.

A FIRST THANKSGIVING DINNER

By Jeannette Young

Use a bare polished dining table, or, if that is impossible, use a heavy brown linen cover with deep hem. Lay across it two bead-work strips eighteen inches wide, such as come for decorative purposes, placing one lengthwise and one crosswise, and under each plate put a doily of canvas and bead work; the candelabra placed at the corners are to have red shades and red candles.

The centerpiece is an Indian pottery jar, filled with eagle and peacock feathers. A little bark canoe on either side is filled with red apples. Over the table is stretched a canopy of bandanna silk, in rich reds and tans, held to the ceiling by a wooden war shield and at the four corners by spears.

The electric bulbs should be covered with red silk to give the effect of candle and firelight shining over all. There might be several musicians in Pilgrim costume, with guitar and mandolins to play through dinner, also a pretty girl in Indian dress to give away souvenirs of bead bags, belts and chains, Indian baskets, moccasins, tiny bows and arrows and little canoes.

The china should be the old English ivory and blue ware, but the Chinese gray and white go well with this color idea, as well as silver and cut glass. With the gay, picturesque coloring of the scene and the guests in simple gowns, it is a very effective dinner party. The ladies may dress Pilgrim fashion, in simple gray cotton crepe gowns and fichus, dainty cuffs, aprons and caps of white, and buckled shoes, the men in gray or black knee breeches, doublet and hose.

The dinner cards should be of birch bark. Now comes the menu, which is of great interest and importance also. First we serve oyster cocktails, perfectly chilled, then cream of tomato soup with dainty croutons. Baked red snapper or salmon with oyster sauce, potato croquettes, roast turkey, cranberry sauce, saddle of venison, scalloped potatoes, roast duck, creamed asparagus, celery, olives, currant jelly, salted nuts, frozen punch, lobster salad, chicken salad, rye sandwiches, cheese straws, Indian suet pudding, brandy sauce, maple ice cream, bonbons, coffee.

A HARVEST DINNER

By Linda Hull Larned

The time was late in September, the occasion a county fair, the place a town in one of the far western states, and the episode a prize dinner table in one of the departments roped off for the exploits of women. But no one in the effete east could ever hope to offer anything quite so attractive, and this particular corner was more besieged by the masculine element than any other exhibit on the grounds. Of course, women were there in throngs, for in spite of new-fangled notions they are ever eager to encourage the efforts and applaud the success of those of their own sex who thus honor their especial vocation.

Among several displays of dinner table settings, this won the prize, because it was not only extremely unique and deliciously dainty, but because it was appropriate to the occasion, and exceedingly practical and easy of accomplishment by anyone with one whit of artistic ability. In fact, the fame of this particular episode has gone far afield, for New York and Boston have since endeavored to imitate its simple splendor, until now the "farm dinner" has grown to be quite the fad.

The Table Decorations

It was an oval, damask covered table, quite large enough to seat twelve comfortably. People in September need plenty of elbow room, for they are just in from a summer "all out of doors." The center decoration was composed of a promiscuous gathering of the brightest and shiniest of vegetables in season, all massed in artistic confusion. These rested on a bed of autumn leaves, and were capped by a huge pumpkin made into a Janus-faced jack-o'-lantern. The leaves circled themselves into slim small bottomed figure 8's toward the end of the table, and these end rings were garnished with fruits, while smaller double-faced pumpkin lanterns surmounted their middles. There were four large gourd cucumbers hollowed out into boat shape, and these were also carved into long-drawn, awe-inspiring faces. They were propped up against the pile of vegetables and formed the corner sentinels to this bulwark of garden produce.

Of course the center pumpkin man's body was a box, which raised him above his fellows, and yet its mission was entirely concealed by masses of kale and endive, and both red and green cabbage leaves, which formed the background for the following vegetables: potatoes, small cabbages and cauliflower, both well trimmed, turnips, parsnips, carrots, crooked neck squash, green corn and tomatoes. String beans, yellow egg tomatoes, radishes, brussels sprouts, okra buds and nasturtium vines formed the buds and tendrils for this autumn banquet. Many of these were cut so as to show only a suggestion of their character, and they were all spick and span clean. The end wreaths held apples, grapes, melons, plums, peaches, pears and an occasional orange. The apples and pears were cut in two the long way, so as to show their seeds and luscious white interiors.

In the middle of the fruit mounds, on the outside ends, were two more jack-o'-lanterns, made from scooped-out eggplants, and their dark, reddish purple faces shone with pleasure at the delightful proximity of creamy red and white lady apples and pale green hothouse grapes. Nasturtium blossoms were tucked into every crevice, and their golden yellow petals glittered like flecks of hot sunshine left over from the summer.

There were corsage bouquets for the women made of
deep, rich red dahlias tied with ribbon grass, and for
the men boutonnieres of small but perfect sunflowers.
The china, glass and silver were moderate in tone and
quality, so as not to disturb the harmony of this harvest
symphony, the glass all fine engraved crystal, and the
china the old-fashioned plain, gilt-banded white so much
used in our grandmothers' day.

The room in which this festive board was laid was
in utter darkness, and yet the effect was sufficiently
luminous, as from each pumpkin man's face shone rays
from the numerous candles or electric lights within, and
the cucumber corners and eggplant ends sent forth
enough more light to render the occasion one of weird
festivity.

Of course in these days of practical education, no
county fair is complete without its food demonstrator,
therefore this menu bore the hall mark of an expert,
for it was delicious, and yet withal economical. The
guests were the "personages" who usually descend upon
every public gathering in order to give the proper tone
to the occasion. This especial festivity was graced by
his excellency, the lieutenant-governor, and his wife,
and just a few ordinary mortals, who were, nevertheless,
county dignitaries. The entire affair was in charge of
a committee of the woman's department, which was ably
marshaled by the aforesaid domestic science specialist,
and many of the good things they prepared were composed of the interior of the decorations, while the
remainder was of things in season, consequently not

expensive, thus setting an example of thrift and economy not to be despised in these days of high-priced provender.

The Various Dishes

The appetizing beginning was an "autumn canape" —slices of toast of uniform size spread with a paste of mashed cucumber and mayonnaise dressing, profusely sprinkled with minced green peppers and nasturtium pods. A seasonable soup was "brussels sprouts consomme." Everyone knows that brussels sprouts are only Lilliputian cabbages, but their delicacy of flavor compensates for their diminutiveness. One quart of them were simply boiled in salted water, then drained into the hot consomme. As this particular county was in close proximity to one of our inland seas, "lake trout fillets with Michigan sauce" was the next course. This trout was skinned, boned and cut into small pieces the moment it was caught. It was covered with a marinade of olive oil, vinegar, salt and pepper until the time arrived for it to be cooked; it was then drained, sprinkled with salt and pepper, dredged with corn meal and sauted in bacon fat until a golden brown all over. It was then served with a spoonful of cold sauce on each fillet, the sauce being mayonnaise dressing mixed with minced capers, cucumbers and tomatoes, and fresh horse-radish grated fine. A dish of fried potato straws was then passed, and so were tiny sandwiches of brown bread and butter. The *piece de resistance* which followed was "roasted ducks," stuffed with mashed potato,

minced onion fried in bacon fat, and chopped celery.
With this was served a souffle of eggplant and squash,
which was boiled, then mashed and mixed with soft
bread crumbs, beaten egg, lemon juice, melted butter,
salt and pepper. This was baked and served in a large
silver vegetable dish, and with this course was also
served a dish of homemade noodles, boiled, drained,
seasoned with butter, salt and pepper, and covered with
a sprinkling of Italian cheese, finely grated. Also, for
the sake of tradition, I suppose, a homely, but excellent
dish of green corn on the cob. It was deliciously sweet
and tender and the ordinariness of it was completely
redeemed by the manner in which it was served. It
came in concealed by a peculiar shaped napkin of white
linen embroidered in yellow maize designs, and every
kernel was scored before sending it to the table, which
made it possible to scrape it from the cob with a fork.
After this, directly from the field close by, were
"steamed fresh mushrooms." The big ones were baked
after being stuffed with the little ones, which had been
mixed with salt and pepper and butter. They were
then deluged with cream and each one served on its own
piece of toast covered with a glass cup.

Then a much-needed respite was taken, during
which the guests cooled their palates with a muskmelon
sherbet. The muskmelons were small ones cut into
halves, each being filled with a lemon ice, colored leaf
green and garnished with bits of angelica. This cool
bit of lusciousness stimulated the palate of the guests
sufficiently to enable them to go on with the feast, and

they were quite ready for the medley of vegetables which was called a "harvest salad." Upon investigation this was found to be composed of small pieces of tomatoes, celery, green peppers and sour apples mixed with French dressing. This was arranged on plates with lettuce leaves. Each one was capped by a tiny mold of cucumber jelly and garnished around the edge with yellow egg tomatoes cut into quarters. With this course were hot crackers covered with Young America cheese grated and mixed with butter, vinegar, English mustard and Wiesbaden sauce. The cucumber jelly was made by boiling some more of the cucumber insides with a little onion and parsley, then adding half a box of gelatine dissolved, a little tarragon vinegar, salt and plenty of paprika, to each pint of liquid. The dessert was another descent to the everyday rations of Auld Lang Syne, but everyone, even the most fastidious, ate with gusto one little

Golden Pumpkin Pielette

These were made after the old New England recipe, but baked in individual tins, then removed and served on white and yellow plates supported by nothing more substantial than a dainty yellow and white paper doily. In all well-regulated families this would have been the last course, but as this was an extraordinary function the mounds of "peaches and wheat parfait" were greeted as enthusiastically as any that had gone before. These were made of boiled custard mixed with a small quantity of a powdered preparation of wheat, to which was added when cold its bulk in whipped and sweetened cream, and a flavoring of peach and almond extract. This was poured into ordinary coffee cups upon halves of peaches, then packed in ice and salt. When served they were sprinkled with powdered sugar and garnished with peach leaves.

This entire menu, with the exception of the *piece de resistance,* was served from the side by the capable assistants of the demonstrator, who were also the "committee." The "judge" was invited to be master of ceremonies, and it was evident that he had had much experience by the skillful manner in which he manipulated the ducks. With the tiny cups of French coffee came the call for toasts, and the judge again showed his knowledge of the fitness of things by immediately squelching the facetious guest who demanded that the "demonstrator" be called upon to give them a "milk toast."

ARTISTIC DINNER DECORATIONS

By Mary Putnam

For a successful geranium dinner, the hostess carried out a scheme of her own. Down the center of the table extended a long, narrow box, or succession of boxes, of stiff cardboard. Geranium cuttings, each bearing large red blossoms and bedded in wet tissue paper, filled the boxes. The sides of this box arrangement were banked, so to speak, with fine ferns. This was done by building up a sand bank, on a paper surface, against the box, and sticking the ferns in the sand. The red of this novel centerpiece was matched in the bill of fare with tomato bisque soup and the dash of color which maraschino cherries gave to the whipped cream surmounting parfait glasses of chocolate ice. The ice, the cream and the cherries were a symphony in brown, red and white.

Everybody was in clover at the dinner with this designation, for it was an engagement dinner, and in the huge round dish on the table were almost clovers enough to hide the blooming fiancee in its pink florescence. Radiating from the bouquet were pink ribbons, each ending in a heart, made for the occasion and bearing a highly sentimental motto. The guests tugged at the hearts until the ribbon ends were drawn from out the bouquet, and attached to one ribbon was found a ring. This, of course, betokened the early engagement of the girl who drew it. Big clover blossoms and leaves were pinned on the lamp shades, and the cards were decorated with tiny cupids. Strawberry sherbet of a decidedly pink hue was served in tall parfait glasses, topped with whipped cream and fresh strawberries.

For the birthday of a dainty college girl, the sweet pea was chosen as the flower for table decorations, the sweet pea in enchanting profusion. In the center of the table was a tall vase of beautiful favrile glass, containing sweet peas and heaped about with bunches of sweet peas in a veritable little mountain, almost three feet in diameter. There were three or four dozens of the peas in each bunch. From this fairy structure trailed ribbons, starting with great, luxuriant bows. The guests received dinner favors of stickpins of sweet pea design, pink and white.

The prettiest dinner of all was the buttercup. A great bouquet of buttercups shed its glory over the round table and the entire room. The big brass dish which held it was encircled at a distance of about eight inches with a row of smilax, and outside this was a fringe of the flat leaves of the jonquil, all of the same size, like a conventional pattern. Narrow ferns might take the place of the jonquil leaves at a later season. At the plates were bunches of jonquils. The candles and the lamp shades were yellow.

A CHINESE DINNER

By Harriet Quimby

An invitation recently sent out by a this season's debutante provoked the keenest of delight among her

THE MENU CARD WRITTEN IN CHINESE

half dozen favored friends, who, after examining the dainty water color sketch of a Chinese belle in gay attire, like a gorgeous butterfly poised for a moment on the corner of the card, read: "Will the most beautiful daughter of the Hon. S— accept the solicitation of her humble and unimportant friend to join in the gathering of the gracious daughters and partake of the most ancient and blessed blossom feast to which the gods of our fathers have given sanction. On the eighteenth hour of the ninth day of the first month."

A Chinese luncheon or dinner suggests more novel decorations than almost any other. It can be given at a cost of fifty cents per plate, or the estimate may easily run up to the fifty-dollar mark. The decorations may be simple and picturesque; in fact, the gay colors needed to give atmosphere can be purchased for a few cents. For a more substantial repast than a flower feast, chop suey or a pineapple chicken may be added to the menu.

If the invitations are for the afternoon, the curtains should be drawn and a few Chinese lanterns—red is the most characteristic color—hung here and there in the dining room, give a mysterious, subdued effect. Chinese incense (sandalwood is the best) can be bought for a few cents. A small dish of charcoal is needed. Upon this lay, kindling wood fashion, a few squares of the sandalwood. After a moment's contact with the coal, a slender column of perfumed smoke will curl in ascending spirals, filling the air with a pleasing fragrance. Punk is also pleasing, but not so dainty as the sandalwood. However, if the latter is used, a small orange suspended by a wire may be filled, the wooden ends of the incense thrust in the fruit, as many as the space will allow. Each lighted, and the glowing ball swinging directly over the table, lends a quaint oriental effect. A girl clever with tissue paper can make a few branches of cherry or plum blossoms, using real twigs and fastening the blossoms with paste. The hostess may or may not be attired in Chinese costume, but when she prepares the blossom dessert, as she may do at table with the chafing-dish, she will make a far more fascinating picture gowned in the charming frock of Ah Chee ("golden branches").

If she learns a few ceremonious phrases and assumes a flowery speech for the afternoon, the fun will be the greater.

The first course of an oriental dinner is tea served in tiny bowls. To make this perfectly, the boiling water must first be turned in the bowl to warm it, then back to the kettle. The tea leaves are then thrown in the bowl, the water poured over, and it can be served immediately. This is sipped from the bowl. Next a preserve of some kind is served. If in the city, where the Chinese preserved fruits can be bought, then *gun got* (preserved limes), ginger, called *town gong,* or *sir lee* (sweet pears) may answer. But if the hostess wishes to preserve the Chinese appetizer herself, then she may buy at any fruit stand the small Chinese mandarin: Cut the peel down in lily form, leaving the bottom whole and the white on top exposed. Drop these into boiling water, cook until tender. Have prepared in a porcelain kettle a thick syrup of white sugar and water. Boil until a drop in cold water has the consistency of wax. Then drop in the oranges, put on the back of the stove and let simmer for half an hour. Take out, let dry in the oven until the surface is glazed. This not only is a very artistic preserve, but a delicious one. Chinese nuts are very good with this.

If soup is desired, a chicken mushroom soup is very nice and more apt to be relished than birdsnest or shark fins. Boil a young chicken until a rich stock is made, into this put half a dozen water chestnuts shaved thin to give flavor; a bit of chopped ham, salt, pepper. Cut some of the white meat into dice, let all boil together twenty minutes. Mushrooms may be added. Just before serving, beat two eggs lightly and stir them in. Sprinkle with chopped parsley and serve immediately.

Chop Suey—For six persons. One pound of water chestnuts; two pounds of bean sprouts, which can be procured at any Chinese vegetable stand. While shopping, buy a quarter's worth of *gee yow,* a Chinese sauce made only in China, and which enters into nearly all oriental meat dishes. It is a brown looking liquid with a peculiar flavor and can be purchased of any Chinese dealer. The water chestnuts must be shaved thin; add a little sliced celery, one small onion chopped, half a dozen mushrooms; cut young chicken into small pieces. Have a kettle with peanut oil (in same quantity as lard would be used), into this place the vegetables and chicken all together. Let fry until tender, stirring often to prevent burning. Just before taking off add the bean sprouts, which must not cook too long, as they are better when little more than half done. Drain off the liquor, add a little flour to thicken; salt to taste. Just at the last add a teaspoonful of the brown sauce. Pour all over the chop suey, stir together and serve.

Pineapple Fish—A dish recently introduced in New York and much relished by the epicure. Take a fresh fish, pike preferred, remove bones, cut in inch squares. Make a batter of egg and flour; dip the squares of fish until well covered, and drop in smoking hot peanut oil until a dainty brown. Let dry in the oven until vegetables are prepared. Chop a little celery, one small green onion, about five mushrooms and one small can of pineapple. Drain off the juice; chop the pineapple into small pieces. Then add the pineapple juice, enough to cover, and boil all together. Just before serving, drop in the squares of fish. Carry to table piping hot.

This is a dainty condiment in which the fish takes on a delicious flavor from the pineapple and defies analysis as to just what kind of meat it is.

To prepare squab *a la* Chinese, boil whole in salted water until half done; take out, dry with napkin; drop into a pot of peanut oil as for doughnuts and brown slowly. The Chinese do not make bread; rice is eaten with every course. Sometimes, however, a sort of biscuit is served. To make these, mix as for ordinary biscuit. Prepare chopped ham, a bit of parsley, chopped onion, a few mushrooms; then take mixture about the size of a walnut, wrap the dough around it and steam until done. These are very good served with the pike or with chicken.

Pineapple Chicken—Take a raw chicken and cut

in good sized pieces, fry slowly in peanut oil until done. Take canned pineapple cut in dice, let boil for a moment and add to the chicken with enough juice to make gravy. With the pineapple chicken or with any roast or fried meats (the Chinese never boil meat), a brown salt is given. Common table salt is put in the oven until a rich dark brown. While it is still salt it takes on a different flavor, and is always served with a high-class Chinese dinner.

Chrysanthemum Dessert—Take two eggs, beat lightly; add wheat flour to make thin batter; no salt. Take a fresh chrysanthemum, yellow or white preferred, though any color will do; wash well, then pluck leaves, stir in batter. Chop a little of the green leaf also and add. Stir well together. Have ready smoking hot peanut oil. Take fork, pick up a few leaves out of the batter, drop lightly in oil, brown for a moment and remove to drain on absorbent paper. These may be done in the afternoon. Just before serving, drop again in the oil to make the outside crisp; sprinkle with powdered sugar and serve.

A more dainty dish cannot be imagined than this chrysanthemum conceit, which looks as dainty as it tastes. Rose leaves are prepared in the same way; honeysuckle or violets may be used to lend variety to color; but none are so delightful to the palate as the chrysanthemum. These may be prepared in a short time with the chafing-dish, and for an ordinary afternoon tea, served with champagne wafers, they make a most novel refreshment. If deep red roses are used, the color is beautiful. The drops of yellow chrysanthemums look like buttercups.

For a good Chinese candy, home prepared, to be the last course, and pretty served in little plum blossom favors, take a fresh cocoanut, cut in two-inch strips, boil in syrup until tender; let dry in slow oven and roll in powdered sugar. The Chinese lychee nuts can be purchased anywhere.

Another candy, very nice and in keeping with an oriental dinner, is common potato sliced an eighth of an inch thick. Boil in syrup until almost done; sprinkle well with ginger; let dry in a slow oven and roll in powdered sugar before serving. It is very difficult for one uninitiated to say what this candy is, yet it is very appetizing and exceedingly wholesome.

FOR A BIRTHDAY

By B. P.

An openwork cut silver fern dish, filled with exquisite growing ferns (a birthday gift), and the possession of a grandmother with silver candlesticks, which she is willing to lend, gave the *motif* for the silver and pink decorations of the table to be described. Even the bonbons were encased in silver foil and the frosting on the cake was imbedded with infinitesimal silver candies—dragees, in confectioner's parlance. A genial glow was shed over the table by light coming through pink candle shades, and this color was accentuated by bunches of large, long-stemmed roses placed at each plate, eight in each rose holder.

* * * * "Who dreams without their thorns of roses?" Verily, she who makes the holders, and they who receive the roses in them! For by this device the flowers can be handled with*out* care! A flat pattern of the holder is given, with measures and directions for

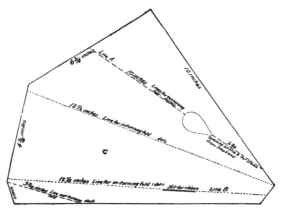

folding. The material to be used is rough, medium-weight water-color paper, the edges picked and torn unevenly in imitation of handmade paper, and a border of liquid silver is applied to both back and front; ornament further if you wish with silver scroll work, but leave the large out-turning flap plain. Lay the flowers along the space marked C; the stems are to go through the opening in line A, and be kept in place by a ribbon

(in this case a wide, soft pink one) which passes over
them, through the slit in the line B, and ties in an
artistic bow. The large flap is reserved for a quotation,
printed in silver as prettily as may be. The finished
affair is not put at the place of the person "to whom it
most concerns," but is carefully laid for somebody else.
When the guests leave the table at the end of the dinner,
each one gives his bunch of roses to the one for whom
he thinks the quotation most fitting; there is seldom
any mistake, if the hits are palpable to the undiscerning,
as they should be; it is no place for a delicate analysis
of character. The sentiments naturally vary with the
occasion and the age of the participants. The personal
quotation idea at a dinner is generally a success; but as
an imperative factor in making it so, the selections
would better be of a complimentary nature, and never
be hits upon unpleasant facts which could possibly hurt
or offend. It is easy to find dozens of short, pithy
classics in both prose and verse, that are applicable and
"pat." At a family party I attended last year a great
deal of fun came from the use of original squibs,
doggerel and play upon the names, fads and foibles of
its members, which would, however, have but little
suggestion for the general reader. Even in the quotations for the dinner in hand several changes were necessary for publication—but it gives the idea:

> "Well may you always be,
> Ill may you never see,
> Here's to your health,
> And the good companie!"

"One of the few, the immortal names, that were not born to die!"

"The glass of fashion and the mold of form!"

"Full of wise saws, and modern instances."

"He hath prosperous art
  When he will play with reason and discourse,
  And well he can persuade."

"All the world loves a lover!"

"A laugh is worth a hundred groans in any market!"

"The kindest one,—
  The best conditioned and unwearied spirit
  In doing courtesies."

"She was the sweet marjoram of the salad, or rather, the herb of grace."

"Of stature tall—I hate a dumpy woman!"

"You have a nimble wit; I think it was made of Atalanta's heels."

"Thou art thy mother's glass, and she in thee,
  Calls back the lovely April of her prime."

"Her voice was ever soft,
  Gentle and low; an excellent thing in woman."

"Thou pendulum betwixt a smile and tear!"

It is unnecessary to say that the first one went uner-
ringly to the host, and the "immortal" one, without a
quiver of hesitation, to the man who rejoices in the not
unusual cognomen of Smith. The dandy of the company, to his apparent satisfaction, received the third
quotation, and the eighth in the list was given, of
course, to the hostess. Only the kind heart of the
compiler kept her from substituting for number eleven:

"Look, she's winding up the watch of her wit—
bye and bye it will strike!"

it was so distinctly characteristic; but you see, it has
a little sting.

The following menu combined with the table decorations to make what "he whom we delighted to honor"
thought was a fortunate and pleasing effect of color:

Creme de marron   Pulled bread
        Oyster loaf   Celery
  Frogs' legs, fried   Stuffed mushrooms
          Orange punch
Redhead duck   Sweet potatoes with sherry
        Green grape jelly
      String bean salad in ice-block

Welsh sandwiches

Nesselrode pudding   Maraschino sauce

Angel cake   Coffee

Creme de Marron—Boil and blanch three pints of chestnuts. Pound one pint and reserve for the pudding. Return the remaining quart to the kettle and stew tender in enough water to a little more than cover. Press through a fine sieve and add one quart of white stock. Heat to the boiling point and season with salt, pepper, a few drops of nutmeg, onion and celery essence. Lastly add one pint of whipped cream. Color green with a few drops of spinach extract.

Oyster Loaf—I quite envy the woman who serves this dish for the first time, if her guests "fall to" with the same gusto ours did. Prepare a fresh loaf of baker's bread by cutting out a square from one end and tearing out the inside, as whole as possible. When but a shell is left, butter it well inside. Wash and drain a quantity of fine oysters, according to the size of the loaf, and fill it exactly as you would a dish for scalloped oysters, seasoning in layers with butter, pepper and salt, but omitting the crumbs. Replace the end of the loaf, rub the outside lightly with butter, set in a dripping pan and bake for about half an hour—a little longer than in a dish. The loaf will swell enough to keep the "lid" in place. Serve on a long platter in a border of cress. Probably as you try to cut it, it will crush to a savory mass. Make pulled bread of the inside of the loaf and dry in the oven.

Dip the frogs' legs in milk; sprinkle with salt and pepper, roll in flour and cook to a delicate brown in deep, smoking hot fat. Serve on a napkin with

Stuffed Mushrooms—Take off the stalks from fresh, large mushrooms, peel the caps with a silver knife and drop them into cold water to keep them white. If they must stand for some time add a little lemon juice to the water; scrape the stalks, chop, and put into a saucepan with one tablespoonful of butter and a slice of onion; cook slowly for ten minutes, then add a tablespoonful of flour and cook five minutes more; add one cupful of stock and one-half cupful of bread crumbs; season with salt and a dash of cayenne. Fill the mushroom cups with this mixture, sprinkle with buttered crumbs, place on circles of fried or toasted bread about the size of the mushroom, and bake in a moderate oven for fifteen minutes.

Orange Punch—Boil together a quart of water and two and one-half cupfuls of sugar for ten minutes; add the juice of six oranges and one lemon; strain, and when cold add the contents of a pint bottle of champagne, and a very small quantity of damask-rose color paste, and freeze. This quantity, served in punch cups, was enough to put fourteen palates in readiness for

Duck—Pick, singe and wipe outside. Salt and pepper the inside after carefully drawing and wiping out with a piece of old linen. Do not wash them. Cut off the wings at the second joint and truss the duck neatly. Roast in a *very* hot oven from fifteen to twenty minutes, in a baking pan containing a little water; baste frequently. Celery or onions, or apples, cored and quartered, are sometimes placed inside the duck to improve the flavor. The breasts of our duck were removed in the kitchen, whole and hot, and sent to the table, one each on *hot* individual plates, on a small piece of fried hominy.

When "canvasback" or "redhead" are on the menu, the host sometimes prefers to carve at table; in that case it is customary, after drawing the duck, to cut an opening at the neck, and through it pull the head and neck, letting the head emerge at the back between the drumsticks and tying it securely in place. This method of serving says to your guests, "You are eating canvasback, at five dollars a pair," and has the additional objection of giving cold portions, unless the host is an expert carver.

The day following this dinner we had a salad from the meat remaining on the uncarved parts, which I give:

Duck Salad—Cut the duck in small uniform bits, and marinate with a French dressing, substituting orange juice for lemon juice or vinegar. Mix with half the quantity, each, of orange carpels, freed from seeds and skin, and tender bits of celery. Add more dressing and garnish with olives and slices of orange, from which the skin has not been taken.

Sweet Potatoes with Sherry (Miss Farmer)—Bake a dozen medium-sized potatoes till soft, and cut in halves lengthwise. Scoop out the inside, press through a potato ricer, season with butter, salt and a dash of sherry, moisten with cream and put back in the shells, leaving a roughened surface on top. Brown in a hot oven.

An old soldering iron that I have threatened to throw away every spring and fall for—I didn't say how many years!—helped me out in preparing my ice dish. I attempted to freeze an ice bowl in a double mold, with my small freezer, and failed dismally; but "'can do' is an easy thing to carry about with you!" so I took a square block of ice and melted out with my despised soldering iron a shapely hollow, big enough to hold the salad, lined the hollow with lettuce leaves and filled it with a salad of string beans; then set the block of ice on a folded napkin on a large silver tray and garnished the base with lettuce and olives, the latter resting in pink rose leaves.

Welsh Sandwiches—Rub together two parts of soft, mild cheese and one part of butter; flavor with mustard and an herb vinegar, and spread between thin slices of bread, cut in dainty shapes.

Nesselrode Pudding—One half-pint of almonds, chopped and pounded; one pint of chestnuts (prepared as above directed), one half-pint of pineapple, grated; one-quarter of a pound of mixed candied fruits, cut into dice and soaked in two tablespoons each of sherry and maraschino; one-half pint of cream; yolks of five eggs; two teaspoons of vanilla; one-half pint of boiling water and one-half pint of sugar. Boil sugar, water and juice from the pineapple for ten minutes. Beat yolks and add, cooking like a custard. Cool and beat light. Mix nuts and candied fruits with the cream, add the flavoring and a bit of salt, fold into the custard and freeze in the usual way. Serve with a garnish of whipped cream, sprinkled with candied rose leaves, or with

Maraschino Sauce—Beat to a cream the yolks of two eggs and two tablespoonfuls of powdered sugar. Stir over the fire in a double boiler till the egg is slightly thickened; take from the heat and continue to beat till the mixture is cold; it will be light and creamy. Add two tablespoonfuls of maraschino and mix lightly with half a pint of cream whipped to a dry, stiff froth. Serve on the dish with the pudding.

A CHERRY BLOSSOM DINNER

By Grace Hortense Tower

Unique beyond anything that had ever before been given in the social line in Pasadena, California, was a cherry blossom dinner given by T. Aoki, a Japanese artist, in honor of the cherry blossom festival of Japan. For weeks, Aoki and his students, some of them American girls who study with him, had been busy decorating the studio, painting the dinner cards and decorating and writing the cards of invitation, seventy-five of which were dispatched by special messenger three days before the affair was to take place. Six thousand artificial cherry blossoms had been sent from Japan for the embellishment of a large natural cherry tree which occupied the center of the great oval table. Dozens of

THE HOST AND HIS HELPERS PREPARING FOR THE
CHERRY BLOSSOM DINNER

wild goat skins, upon which were wrought most exquisite designs of peonies, iris, cherry blossoms, dragons, storks, demons and gods, covered one wall, while above ran a double frieze of crimson and green matting made of the fiber of the famous Japanese dwarf pine. Clusters of purple wistaria blossoms were painted upon the green, while the stately iris embellished the crimson. Upon the opposite wall were queer Japanese symbols and banners, the massive pillars being inscribed with little love stories and Japanese poems to the cherry tree, following out the pretty Japanese custom of hanging poems upon the blossom-laden trees in the glad springtime.

The windows had been painted to represent a garden of flowers, purple iris, rose-tinted cherry blossoms and graceful wistaria clusters rivaling one another in beauty. The only hint that one was not in a corner of the flowery kingdom was the large silken American flag, whose graceful folds were draped with the flag of Japan from the ceiling over the table.

Scores of odd white lanterns, painted in fleur-de-lis, were caught to walls, pillars and screens, while upon each picket of the little bamboo fence surrounding the "centerpiece" was a pink lantern. A shower of pink petals covered the space beneath the tree, while the tablecloth had been painted an hour or two before the dinner, with huge pink cherry blossoms.

The favors for the ladies were miniature jinrikishas, the typical Japanese vehicle, while tiny china mandarins and gods were given the men. The napkins were of cherry blossom pink tissue paper. The delicate pink

and gold wine cups with an embossed cherry blossom
in the bowl were also given the guests as souvenirs
after they had drunk the host's health in the pungent
rice wine served in them. The menu was as follows:

Consomme peony
Lovers' knot potpourri
Carp fish
Golden epaulets and compound salads
Braised chicken   Spring mushrooms
Royal gems   Pounded fish
Cherry blossom tea
Excellent palace rice
Vegetables carved to represent fleur-de-lis and peonies
Hama   Chidore
Mixed fruits

Six Japanese men deftly and noiselessly served the
dinner, the little host explaining each course as it was
brought in. Suddenly during the course of the meal
there burst upon the air strange wailing notes, weird,
yet sweet, and in a moment Nakamura, another Japanese artist, came in and played to the guests quaint
Japanese lullabies upon his flute—a straight piece of
bamboo hollowed out and as smooth as ivory.

THE "COLD COMFORT DINNER"

By Mary Dawson

Each course at one of these affairs is served cold and the comfort extends equally to hostess, guest and maid. The woman who does not keep a maid can entertain charmingly in this way and without the addition of that final course so often seen in maidless entertaining, of "hot, worn-out hostess." Here are a few "cold comfort" menus in outline. Using these as a basis the busy housekeeper will be able to build up a simple or elaborate bill of fare without much planning.

MENU NO 1

Fruit frappe served in tumblers
Deviled eggs   Cress sandwiches
Cold sliced or jellied tongue   Potato salad
Coffee   Rolls and butter
Individual molds of wine jelly containing candied fruit
Ice cream   Cake   Bonbons

MENU NO 2

Grape fruit
Cold consomme with toasted crackers
Pickled fish
Game in season   Cold sliced ham
Potato salad   Rolls and butter   Currant jelly
Dressed cucumbers in cucumber baskets
Berries   Ice cream   Russes   Coffee

MENU NO 3

Clams
Iced bouillon
Cold salmon   Olive sandwiches
Cold chicken   Stuffed rolls
Hollowed out tomatoes filled with dressed asparagus tips
Hot coffee   Frozen pudding   Iced tea
Wine croquettes

MENU NO 4

Frapped grapes
Cold clam bouillon
Chicken salad   Olives   Rolls and butter
Coffee
Stuffed eggs in lettuce nests
Orange jelly in orange baskets   Ice cream
Cake   Bonbons

AN OMAR KHAYYAM DINNER

By M. C. D.

One of the prettiest ideas developed lately in dinner decorating, which can be carried out by anyone with some skill in drawing, is an Omar Khayyam dinner. The scheme of such a dinner embraces name cards decorated in Persian designs in Persian rug colors, each bearing an appropriate quotation from the Rubaiyat, which abounds with them. The quotations should be done in red on dark brown cards, with the name underneath. In the center of the table a large irregularly cut skin in brown or dark red, which can be purchased for a dollar in any of the art shops, should be placed, and on this a pot full of deep red roses. The pot, of course, refers to the Rubaiyat lines on the potter, and, let it be whispered, the family bean pot will be picturesque, if no other is available.

A LITERARY DINNER

By M. C. D.

At a dinner given by a literary woman in honor of a literary man, the menu and flowers were not unusual, but the name cards were. At each place the hostess had laid a rejection slip of one of the prominent magazines or newspapers. These were all mounted on large fancy pasteboard cards, so that the symmetry of the table was preserved and on the plain margins the name of the guest who was to occupy the place had been written. The guests, most of whom were contributors, saw the joke at once and all laughed over the merry conceit. Then the rejection slips were read and a vote taken as to which one embroidered its rejection with the most skill. A similar idea was put into effect at the Bohemian club in San Francisco, where a New York editor was entertained by a number of western writers. The tablecloth was entirely covered with rejected manuscripts, their pages being scattered loosely over the cloth.

A TOY DINNER

By Mary Dawson

A toy dinner for grown-up people is a new and fascinating idea for entertaining formally around Christmas season. The table centerpiece is a Christmas tree from the toy shop, trimmed as if for a child's party. Each guest, as he sits down, finds at his cover a plaything in place of a favor. The toys are chosen to fit the hostess' pocketbook. If economy is an object, woolly lambs, jacks-in-boxes, dolls, et cetera, are used. If there is no particular financial limit, mechanical toys are good fun. One ingenious hostess who entertained a Christmas dinner last year inserted a clause in her invitations asking each man or woman to come bringing the most ingenious mechanical toy that could be secured to compete in a contest. The toys were unwrapped between courses at dinner. Afterward, in the drawing room, each owner exhibited his toy. A general vote was taken up to decide which was the cleverest. Each player voted for any except his own by dropping a signed ballot into a box held by the hostess. Prizes were awarded for those toys for which most votes were cast.

THE GUESTS AT A PRETTY DINNER FOUND AT THEIR
RESPECTIVE PLATES LETTERS STANDING, EASEL
FASHION, SO AS TO SPELL THE NAME OF THE CLUB
TO WHICH THEY BELONGED.   THE LETTERS WERE
CUT OUT OF CARDBOARD AND WERE DECORATED IN
WATER COLORS, THIS DUTCH MAIDEN BEING A
LIGHT BLUE.

LUNCHEONS AND TEAS

LUNCHEONS AND TEAS

A SPRINGTIME LUNCHEON

By Anne Warner

ONE bleak and tearful day in early April this simple and dainty board was laid, beguiling a few guests into a belief in the existence of the April that we long for and read about, and which, in our climate, is seemingly a sad laggard. Yet the pussy willows used in decorating had been gathered a few days before when March had "gone out like a lamb."

The center of the antique table of polished mahogany held, on a square of Armenian drawn work, a low iridescent glass vase, yellow and green tones predominating. The vase was filled with salt, and into this foundation the willow twigs were crowded and kept firmly in place. Upon the pussies a cloud of yellow butterflies had apparently alighted and were balancing airily. One of these "winged flowers" poised on the edge of each tumbler and served as a place card and souvenir. Everyone saw at once, of course, that they were paper and in the same instant wondered how they could "fly." The trick is a simple and pretty one. The coloring and shape are approximately those of the clouded sulphur butterfly—the common "puddle butterfly" of our childhood—which sits every summer in swarms in moist spots and makes the wayside gay with the flash of yellow wings. One poor *colias philodice* was sacrificed to be a guide in markings and shadings.

Outline the pattern on the thinnest torchon board (torchon paper is not heavy enough) and paint in water color in broad washes. Use transparent colors, lemon yellow for the center of the wings; a pale tint of Venetian red for the beautiful outer edges of same, and vandyke brown and black for the peculiar markings between. The two "eyes" on the upper wings should be black and those on the lower ones a deeper tint of pinkish red. A faint wash of pale green and a few veinings in the shadows improve the lower wings. The body is painted dark as in nature. When dry, cut out with sharp scissors, carefully following the outline.

Get a small quantity of buckshot F F and hie thee with it to a machine shop where jobbing is done and where an amiable and patient man will follow orders. Experiments showed that the best way to flatten the shot is in a vise. If a piece of one-sixteenth steel be fastened between the jaws of the vise the shot can, one by one, be compressed to a uniform thickness and will be about three-eighths of an inch in diameter. (I feel quite important giving instructions about a vise, inasmuch as I never even saw one before this experience— or, at least, not one spelt with an "s.")

With a little fish glue fasten one of these weights very near the end of the elongated point of each upper wing. To make still more secure, and for the sake of neatness, cover the lead with a circle of white tissue paper, using in this case one of the white pastes that come in tubes; these dry quickly and do not discolor. On placing the head of the insect on the tip of the finger, or on any support not too slippery, it will be found to balance perfectly if directions have been followed. The position gives the butterfly a singularly lifelike appearance, which is enhanced by a slight swaying and waving motion caused by every draft of air.

Bunches of single sweet-scented yellow jonquils in hall and living rooms made spring in the house. Two or three of the same blossoms—stemless—floated in opalescent fingerbowls on a side table. Gold and white china was used so far as practicable, and a few pussy twigs ornamented the plates of the first course, which was on the table when the guests sat down.

MENU

Oyster relish
Celery   Sandwiches
Whitebait
Mush souffle   White radishes
Chicken timbales   Stuffed eggs   Rolls
Washington salad   Imperial sticks
Pineapple in shell   Sweet sandwiches
Filled dates   Oranges glace
Cafe au lait

Blessings truly brighten as they take flight. The housekeeper hunts celery now with as keen a zest as if her family had not nibbled it with relish all winter; we enjoy oysters better than ever when we realize how near is the first "r"-less month. Yet with what avidity do we grasp at any new way of offering old standbys. Oysters are never better than on the half shell, but the arrangement here given has the advantage of novelty.

Make shallow cups by cutting small shaddocks in halves crosswise and removing the pulp; fill with fine oysters and a very few bits of pulp, and lightly cover with a white cap of dressing made of three tablespoons of grated horse-radish root, one tablespoon of vinegar, one-quarter teaspoon of salt and a little paprika—"the goddess of good digestion"; add last of all four tablespoons of cream whipped stiff. Cups, oysters and dressing should be thoroughly chilled and the dressing prepared and put on only at the latest possible moment. An excellent way to send the cups to table is to half bury them in shaved ice. The cups used at this luncheon were prepared three days beforehand and had been kept fresh under water, the pulp having been appropriated for a salad at a previous affair. One can save both work and material by a little forethought.

Look over and wash the tiny fish with great care and rub dry in an old soft napkin. When everything is in readiness, roll in flour a sufficient number to cover the bottom of a fine-meshed wire basket and immediately immerse in smoking hot fat. It takes but a moment to cook them. Turn on to a paper and sprinkle with salt. Let the fat get up to the right temperature while the next "batch" is being floured. Toss them on a sieve to shake off the surplus flour. Serve on a hot napkin on a hotter plate and garnish with a lemon slice

THE SPRING LUNCHEON TABLE, WITH PUSSY-WILLOWS AND YELLOW BUTTERFLIES

which has had the upper side covered with chopped parsley.

They are delicious when attention is given to small details. If you have a cook that you cannot trust to do this, a slice of halibut, cut from the lower part of the fish, makes a good course cooked as follows: Scrape the skin and wipe; season with salt and pepper; lay in a pan and spread the top with a tablespoon each of butter and flour cooked together. Add a few narrow strips of salt pork and broil or bake in a hot oven till brown. Put diagonally across a hot platter and arrange a mound of Parisienne potatoes in one corner and pour a white sauce in the other—garnish same as whitebait. With either the souffle is most appetizing, as it is also with chicken.

Mush Souffle (Mrs Rorer)—Heat one pint of milk; stir in three-quarters of a cup of granulated corn meal and one teaspoon of salt and cook till well scalded. Take from fire and add the yolks of four eggs, one at a time, stirring after each addition. Beat whites of the eggs with a pinch of salt and fold in. Bake twenty minutes in a well-greased baking dish in a quick oven and serve at once. Eat with butter.

The timbales were poached in individual buttered molds decorated with truffles, one tiny can of truffles being enough, and were turned out on the center of a round platter. Arranged about them in a circle were the eggs, and a thin, rich Allemande sauce was poured round the whole.

Stuffed Eggs—Boil six eggs twenty minutes;

remove. shells and cut carefully crosswise. Mash **the** yolks, season with a teaspoon of softened butter, a few drops of onion juice and half the quantity of deviled ham or tongue. Make into balls and fill the white halves. The olives for the course were stuffed with capers.

At this particular luncheon the springlike effect was accentuated by the dishes in which the salad appeared—excellent majolica imitations of romaine leaves—a single one for each person, some of them having an ornament of a very realistic radish. A large dish in this ware, formed of several leaves in a circle curving upward, and a mayonnaise cup, simulating a pale green lettuce heart, make a pretty set for many salads where .the other table appointments are not too elegant.

Washington Salad—Clean, blanch and prepare sweetbreads as usual. Cook in salted, acidulated water containing a slice of onion and a bit of bay leaf; cool and cut in slices. Add half the quantity of sliced cucumbers which have lain in an ice water bath an hour or so and then been dried and seasoned with onion juice, white pepper and salt. Mix with a plain oil dressing, made without mustard. Arrange on individual plates on watercress. Garnish with cucumber as follows: Pare, cut crosswise in thirds or quarters according to size, remove the centers and fill with sauce tartare. Served on a bleached lettuce leaf, this garnish makes a satisfactory little salad by itself.

To make the sticks simply cut bread into long,

slender, uniform fingers, butter lightly and set in a hot oven till a delicate brown. Pile on a plate log cabin fashion. Fry, sprinkling them with grated cheese some time before browning, and eat with bouillon.

One cannot always find a pineapple—large, ripe and unblemished—suitable to serve in this way. The golden-meated juicy variety from Florida is far and away the best that comes to our market. Lacking the perfection that you seek, some other dessert can be substituted—orange cup, for example, with fresh sponge cake. But if you *do* find it, chill, cut off the leafy top, to be used as a cover, and set it aside. Dig out the pulp, taking great care not to puncture the shell, and discarding the fibrous and tasteless core. Add the shredded pulp of another small specimen to replace the waste. Sweeten to taste and keep cold till needed. To serve, fill the shell, fit on the top and set on a dainty doily on a flat china or glass dish. Three butterflies poised on the palmlike top are most effective. The hostess may remove the cover and its decorations intact to another plate and by means of a small ladle, dip the fragrant, luscious fruit on to plates containing each a

Dessert Sandwich—Cut sponge cake into thin oblongs or squares. Put between two pieces a slice of vanilla ice cream that has been molded in brick form. Ornament the top slice of cake with whipped cream (sweetened and flavored slightly with cordial) pressed through a pastry tube.

I give also the recipe for

Orange Cups—Stir over the fire two cups of granulated sugar and one cup of water till dissolved; then let boil without stirring until the syrup spins a thread. Add one pint of orange juice and the juice of one lemon. Scald one cup of cream, stir into beaten yolks of two eggs, cool and mix with the syrup. When thoroughly chilled add another cup of cream whipped, one half a teaspoon of vanilla and touch of yellow color paste. Freeze and serve in glasses.

Salted nuts in small dishes were set at each cover. The dates were stuffed with oblong bits of preserved ginger—an excellent combination. Perhaps a word or two may help those who "never have any luck making glaces." Don't attempt them on a damp day. Divide oranges carefully into sections, rejecting all carpels which have the slightest break in the thin skin; let those that pass muster stand for several hours to dry. Boil the sugar to the point just before the caramel stage and watch closely as it becomes straw colored. Remove to back of range; drop in the orange sections one at a time, take out quickly with two forks, disturbing the syrup as little as possible, and place separately on an oiled marble slab or paper. The syrup will bear reheating once only. Leave a short stem on Malagas and with a pair of pincers take each grape by its handle and dip. Work quickly. Glaces are "peculiar critters" and if the day before they are needed happens to be fine and dry, make them then and keep crisp and fresh under an inverted bowl, which should also cover a small piece of lime.

Mix coffee, eggs and water in the usual proportions,

having the water cold. Set on the range where it will heat, but not boil, for half an hour; then add hot, rich milk, allowing one cup of milk to every quart of coffee. Do not allow to boil.

A CHICAGO LUNCHEON

By Linda Hull Larned

The table was decorated with a big silver bowl of Meteor roses, which, as everyone knows, are a beautiful crimson. The menu was of the following courses:

First, Tokay grapes, ice cold; second, cream soup with breadsticks. This soup was of clams and oysters chopped fine, and tomato juice and pulp mixed with a thin cream sauce, then strained and served in cups with a spoonful of whipped cream in each. Third, creamed scallops and mushrooms. There was an addition of minced truffles, and it was served in ramekin dishes with slices of hard-boiled egg and bits of parsley as a garnish. With this course was a plate of entire wheat bread sandwiches. Fourth, grape fruit sherbet, a creamy orange ice surrounded with a half frozen syrup made of grape fruit juice and sugar. Fifth, chicken fillets, rice balls, French beans, jam.

The chicken breasts were parboiled slightly, then browned under the fire and served with a rich brown sauce, to which the rice balls were added. The rice balls were very tiny but savory, with cheese and salt and lots of paprika. They were fried in deep fat. The beans were the red kidney variety, and as they were canned they were simply warmed in butter, minced parsley and a few drops of lemon juice. The jam was a relish made of rhubarb, strawberries, pineapple, raisins and almonds.

The sixth course was salad macedoine. This was lettuce, grape fruit, celery, apples and white grapes garnished with cream cheese balls flanked by pecan nuts. Over this was a French dressing made with grape fruit juice instead of vinegar. With this were served some tiny sandwiches made of gluten crackers, put together with butter and bar-le-duc jam. The seventh course was rose ice cream and pasties, a French ice cream served in champagne glasses, a spoonful in each, over which was poured a deep pink sauce made of syrup, whipped cream and rum, colored with cochineal.

Upon each plate was an American Beauty rose, which matched the syrup in the glass. Small crescents of puff paste were covered with a meringue upon which were sprinkled blanched and browned almonds minced fine, and the pasties were then slightly browned in the oven. The accessories were salted pecan nuts, popcorn and crimson and white peppermints. Of course the finish was strong black coffee in the tiniest of cups and a thimbleful of creme de menthe for each guest.

FOR INDEPENDENCE DAY

By L. A. Browne

The complaint has often been made by very young ladies, and frequently by older young ladies, that the

Fourth of July was a day much more enjoyed by boys and young men than by the members of their sex. There are ways, however, in which the young lady may both enjoy and celebrate the occasion. An Independence day party is one of these.

Once assembled at the home of the hostess, the guests may enjoy themselves by any of the customary methods adopted by young ladies upon such occasions. They should, however, wear some patriotic emblems, such as red, white and blue sashes or ribbons, and a very pleasant feature of the occasion would be for each guest to come prepared, by request, to give some information regarding the women of Revolutionary times. The crowning feature of the event should be the lunch. The room in which this is served should be well decorated with flags and bunting of the national colors, while such Revolutionary pictures as George and Martha Washington, the battle of Bunker Hill, the Boston tea party, Washington crossing the Delaware, the signing of the Declaration of Independence, the surrender of Cornwallis, etc., should adorn the walls if they are obtainable. The table should be draped about the edge with tri-colored bunting and a knot of this or a flag draped about each chair. If possible, secure a well-mounted American eagle to place in the center of the table, with a flag draped about the base.

At each plate place a paper or muslin flag for a napkin, and upon each plate mount a formidable cannon, made by securing two oranges and a banana with a long wooden or metal pin. A tiny flag stuck

in the lower end of the banana will add to the effect.
The menu should have at the top a flag, either a real one
fastened on or one put on with colors. At the bottom
a drawing of the cracked Liberty bell would be in keeping with the idea, while at either side attach a genuine
firecracker. The lunch menu may be either printed or
written, and should read as follows:

Patriotic sandwiches

Ham and tongue, a la Valley Forge

Star cookies and stripe cake

Pinwheels   Washington pie

Giant firecrackers

Cannon   Torpedoes

Iced tea (without tax)

Pink lemonade, a la July 4

The patriotic sandwiches should be small, dainty
sandwiches tied with red, white and blue ribbons. The
meats, "a la Valley Forge," would of course be cold.
Star-shaped frosted cookies and layer cake explains the
next item. A slice of jelly roll is an excellent imitation
of a pinwheel. Deep pink strawberry ice cream, made
in molds with a shred of cocoanut fuse, makes the giant
firecracker. Put confectionery in small bags or tinfoil
and over this twist red tissue paper in imitation of torpedoes. The cannon has already been described. The
Washington pie and iced tea need no comment. Serve a
straw with the lemonade and in the straw place a tiny
flag. The napkins and menu cards will make good souvenirs for the guests.

A display of fireworks in the evening, superintended by some male member of the family, together with patriotic songs, would be a fitting finale for the occasion, and it is safe to assume that such a celebration would be thoroughly enjoyed by the young ladies.

The older ones would also find this lunch menu suitable, or they could give a dinner party and reception or social hop. For the dinner party the menus should be decorated like the one already described, and contain the following. For the United States soup any light stock will do. Into this place a quantity of macaroni letters "U" and "S." Macaroni now comes stamped out in all the letters of the alphabet. Turkey is of course our native bird. The giant firecrackers, pinwheels, cannon, torpedoes and lemonade have been previously described. The menu:

United States soup

Red sliced tomatoes   White iced cucumbers

Blue cabbage cold slaw

Plymouth Rock cod

Spanish mackerel (done brown)

New England trout

Roast sirloin of American beef

Roast lamb (U S) mint sauce

Our native bird

Washington pickles

Boiled and mashed new potatoes   New beets

Green peas   Indian corn on the cob

White bread   American cheese   Vermont butter

Indian pudding   Washington pie
Pinwheels   Giant firecrackers
Cannon   Torpedoes
Tea (without tax)   California coffee
Pink lemonade, a la July 4

A UNIVERSITY LUNCHEON

By G. W.

A Yale luncheon given last Christmastide was a
brilliant success. The ideas may be utilized for the
entertainment of students from any college, merely
changing the colors, Harvard's crimson, for example,
Iowa's old gold, Chicago's maroon, Texas's white and
orange, or Dartmouth's green. The invitations read:

Miss Rachel Wynn
Miss Frances Sutherland
Mr. Richard Sutherland
Yale Luncheon, 1 o'clock, December 27
Whist from 3 to 6

415 Ayres Avenue

The Wynn house is small. There is a cozy reception hall,
parlor, sitting room and dining room on the first floor.
All the rooms open into each other with wide arches,
which fit it capitally for entertaining. Our decision
was to have no flowers, not even a palm, and keep the
entire house in harmony of coloring. Fortunately for
our scheme, every room had a quiet gray or bluish paper,

and in carpets, furniture and hangings there was not a touch of color that would clash with the blue of Yale. Our first bit of luck was the loan of a huge bundle of Yale flags and bunting from the College Men's club. A flag, with a great white "Yale" on it, we stretched across one end of the sitting room, another, as immense as a campaigning banner, draped the west wall of the dining room. The stairs were garlanded with dark blue bunting, and all over the house fluttered little class flags bearing dates that ran from '80 to '04. We allowed bunches of mistletoe tucked cunningly under gas fixtures. Holly was out of the question; it would have rooted for Harvard.

Serving luncheon at 1 was an innovation, but an excellent one. When the dishes were cleared away the anxiety was over, and the hostess moved about among her guests without a thought of a meal to be served at the end of the game. We set ten small tables, three in the dining room, four in the sitting room, two in the parlor and one in the hall. The tables were snowily linened, there were doilies in blue and white, and the centerpiece on each table was a glass dish filled with small bunches of splendid blue and white grapes. There was nothing blue to be found in the fruit or flower kingdom except these, and the coloring was superb. All the dishes we used were handsome old-fashioned willow ware or solid dark blue.

Blue seems one of the impossible colors to achieve in cooking or garnishing. Where it could not be obtained we used white. Here is the menu served:

Cream of corn soup
Olives   Toasted wafers
Smelts in potato straw nests
Chicken a la Stanley   Sweet potato croquettes
Finger rolls
Grape fruit and celery salad
Cheese straws   Salted almonds
Yale ice cream
Individual angels with Yale icing
Cafe noir

This luncheon was prepared entirely by the young
hostess, her humble right-hand woman, and a cook
girl in the kitchen. During the serving of the meal we
had the aid of a cooking school graduate, who took
general oversight of everything for one dollar an hour.
Two young girls were hired to assist in waiting on the
tables for twenty-five cents an hour. Afterward they
stayed and helped Tenna wash dishes. Service cost
exactly three dollars, and it was as perfect as a caterer
would have charged five dollars for.

The weather was chill enough to allow of much
of the luncheon being prepared the day before. The
vegetable portion of the soup was made and set away to
be combined skillfully at the last moment by the young
woman of cooking school knowledge. The almonds were
salted, the sweet potato croquettes made, egged and
crumbed, the potatoes pared and left in cold water, the
cheese straws and little angels made and the finger rolls
ordered, for at bakeshop prices it is not worth while

troubling with rolls at home. Following are two of the recipes in our menu. Remember of course that each dish provided for forty people.

Yale Ice Cream—A coloring for the ice cream threw the entire household into despair. So far as we could find, there is no blue coloring paste on the market. There is one which produces an adorable violet, only violet is not Yale blue. At last we discovered that a few tablespoons of juice from canned blueberries produced exactly the Yale shade of blue, and added quite a pleasant flavor, which could be accentuated by a dash of lemon extract. We used two freezers, in one making vanilla cream, in the other the Yale mixture. The recipe we used called for two quarts of thin cream, in which was dissolved one and a half cups of sugar. Three tablespoons of vanilla were added to the two quarts of white cream and two tablespoons of lemon for the blue cream. Add the blueberry juice till the cream is quite a dark blue, much bluer than the tint you desire, as all colorings freeze out considerably lighter. The four quarts of cream were packed into brick molds, a layer of blue and another of white, which cut beautifully.

Individual Angels with Yale Icing—A fine frothy mixture of angel cake was baked in small gem pans, and when cool iced with a plain frosting colored by the blueberry juice, and slightly flavored with lemon. A tiny pennant of blue silk with a white Y painted on it was fastened on a slender wire, and stuck in the center of each cake.

While the deft waiters cleared the tables to prepare

for cards, the company spent **fifteen minutes** in merry chat, interspersed with **snatches of Yale** songs. The cards used for playing were blue and white, the score cards bore pretty bits of decoration: the inevitable Yale flag, a football man in a blue sweater, a college crew pulling hard, or a sketchy reminiscence of Yale's famous fence. The lettering was in blue and the tiny pencils attached to each card were of the same color. During the afternoon punch was served from a splendid Delft bowl, and the guests drank from rich blue sherbet cups.

The prizes were exactly of the sort that Yale men and Yale men's girls appreciate, stunning Yale pillows, and a handsome desk pad with a spirited decoration in water color of a football field, where of course the blues were winning. There were blue steins, Yale pins and a blue-bound book designed for holding snapshots of college life. Remembered even to-day are the booby prizes, two Yale brownie jumping jacks, three feet in length, who flung themselves into the most astonishing attitudes when a string was pulled.

The confidential part of the story is that twenty dollars covered the cost of the entire entertainment.

IN MEXICAN STYLE

By O. A. M.

In the following menu all the dishes are such as are cooked in the well-to-do families of Mexico and the households of the Spanish Californians, but several of them are almost unknown to the American epicure who has never crossed the Rio Grande.

The flowers should be in keeping with the menu. A great bowl of yucca blossoms, or a cactus plant in full bloom, would make a pleasing centerpiece; but the flower of all others to choose is the poinsettia, or as the Mexicans call it so prettily, *Luz de Navidad* (the Christmas light), a native of their wild canyons, and the subject of many of their quaint legends.

For place cards nothing would be more appropriate than little sombreros made of gray drawing paper. To make these cut out rounds of paper two and one-half inches in diameter, then make a little cornucopia two inches long for the crown of the hat; notch slightly the mouth of the cornucopia, bend the notches inward and gum them to the round, so that the cornucopia will stand upright in the center of the round. The sombrero is then complete, needing only a hat band of baby ribbon (red). On the upper side of the brim write, in gilt ink, the guest's name, and on the under side of the brim write the menu.

MENU

Sopa de frijoles   Tortillas

Pescades fritos   Mexicano caliente   Olives

Pollo asada   Enchillados   Alcachofada

Chili reinas   Arroz con tomate

Ensalada de aligador pera

Atole de pina   Ojalda

Cafe   Sucre de leche   Fruto

Sopa de frijoles is a puree of the dried red beans. Soak the beans over night, boil till tender in plenty of water, press through a sieve. I find a potato ricer an excellent press for the purpose. Return the beans to the fire with enough of the water they were boiled in to make the amount of soup required, season with cayenne and salt, and thicken slightly with blended flour; strain, and serve with a slice of lemon in each plate. Tortillas are the bread of Mexico, and are served not only with the soup, but with every course, excepting the dessert. The Mexican cook grinds her corn with a *metate* fresh every day, but the American will find the fine white corn meal of the mills will do very well. Mix the meal with a little salt and enough boiling water to make a stiff dough, pinch off a lump the size of an English walnut and pat it between the palms till it becomes a round cake as thin as a wafer and about six inches in diameter. Bake on a griddle, turning it over to bake on both sides. These should be served hot, and may be made the day before using, and heated over when time to serve.

For *pescades fritos,* any dainty variety of fish is boiled in oil, the oil being very hot before putting in the fish. For *Mexicano caliente,* toast in the wood ashes some green peppers and a few red ones (chilis are the peppers used), peel the skins from them: treat an equal quantity of tomatoes in like manner, mince all finely together with a little onion, salt, and vinegar enough to moisten; let stand a few days before using. This is a nice sauce to use with any dishes with which catsup would be suitable.

Pollo asada is roasted chicken, as the Mexicans roast with a spit before the fire. Broiling would be nearer their method than roasting in the oven.

Enchillados are a dish for an epicure. The Mexicans take equal quantities of chilis, tomatoes and onions, but the American will prefer to use only half as much onion, and possibly still less of the chilis, for our northern throats would blister if treated to the fiery seasoning. These should be roasted in the ashes, then peeled, the seeds taken from the peppers, and the whole, excepting the pepper seeds, ground to a pulp. To this add an equal quantity of finely chopped fresh lean pork, and salt to taste. A tortilla is folded around a spoonful of the mixture. When all the mixture is wrapped in tortillas the little bundles are boiled in tomatoes, a little finely chopped raw onion is dusted on top of each, and it is ready for serving.

For *alcachofada,* trim artichoke buds, taking out the chokes, boil till tender in salted water, make a sauce of one cup milk, butter the size of a walnut, or olive oil two tablespoonfuls, one tablespoonful blended flour, and last the beaten yolks of two eggs. Serve a spoonful of sauce with each bud.

Arroz con tomate is a dish without which no Mexican meal is complete. It is rice boiled in tomatoes, after being well plumped in cold water, and seasoned with salt and pepper.

For *chili reinas,* use the large green sweet peppers, roast them in the ashes till they can be easily peeled, then peel, split open on one side, take out the seeds, and stuff the peppers with grated cheese. For six peppers take two eggs, beat very light, add one teaspoonful of flour, dip the peppers in this batter, then fry. When browned on one side, turn. Serve very hot. Pour over them a tomato sauce if wished.

Ensalada de Aligador Pera—Peel alligator pears, cut in thin rings, taking out the stone, serve on lettuce with mayonnaise.

Atole de Pina—Thicken five pints of boiling water with cornstarch until the consistency of boiled custard, add one small pineapple, grated; also one pound sugar, a small stick of cinnamon, and when this has boiled a moment, three very well beaten eggs which have been mixed with a little of the sugar. Stir a moment, then, before the eggs have time to curdle, take from fire, turn into individual custard cups, and serve cold.

Ojalda—Into two cupfuls of flour drop the yolk of one egg, unbeaten, and a heaping tablespoonful of lard. Wet with salted water till a stiff paste is formed, knead well, lifting and throwing it upon the board every moment till it is a light, smooth dough, full of blisters. Roll very thin and cut in rounds. Fry a light brown in hot deep lard, and sift powdered sugar over them as soon as finished. They are crisp and melt in the mouth when well made.

Sucre de Leche—Boil three cups granulated sugar with one cup sweet milk, stir to prevent burning; as soon as it will string from the spoon take from fire, add a little vanilla and pour into buttered pans; cut in cubes.

A CIRCUS LUNCHEON

By Alice Chittenden

The decorations at this unique luncheon carried out as far as possible the idea of a circus. Streamers of white cambric, alternated with wide red ribbons, were festooned from the center of the ceiling in tentlike fashion, thus apparently converting the whole room into a huge circus tent. From the center of this were suspended two paper hoops with dolls dressed like trapeze performers, which were wired to the ceiling as if just about to jump through them. The mural decorations consisted of masks, horns and whips tied with red ribbons. There were ten tables, each of which represented a sideshow at a circus. Some tables were oblong, others round, but the guests were seated on one side only and facing the center.

The floral decorations consisted of poinsettias. To each of the chairs was wired one of these showy blossoms with its beautiful dark green foliage. They were also interspersed among the other decorations on the tables, the snowy cloth making an effective background.

The first table, which was oblong, held a circus procession of animals winding in long spiral ovals its whole length. Only the ingenious young decorators know how many Noah's arks of goodly size (for these were no Lilliputian toys) must have been devastated to furnish the four-footed creatures, to say nothing of the army of dolls required as performers. The chariots were cut from pasteboard and were entwined with flowers.

The second table, a small round one, represented a cannibal island in the Pacific, consisting of a circle of sand and black dolls in gaudy, but scanty, costume. On the third table the chariot races were represented with flower-trimmed chariots and pretty doll drivers who handled the bright ribbons with wonderful skill. The fourth was a small round table, in the center of which a boy doll held the popcorn and peanut concession. On the fifth, trained dogs several inches in hight but of fascinating exterior, were performing on ladders and beating drums under the guidance of a perfectly appointed ringmaster.

Indian snake charmers performed with realistic paper snakes on the sixth. The seventh held a merry-go-round, while at the eighth dainty maidens danced about a maypole. At the ninth, the hoop performance of the ceiling was repeated on a smaller scale, while at the tenth a company of rough riders held sway.

Just before the end of the dinner the beautiful little daughter of the hostess passed around confetti among the guests, showering it upon the guest of honor. Each guest carried away one of the toys as a souvenir, which still left a goodly number behind.

There are suggestions in this dinner which may enable housekeepers to devise attractive feasts on a smaller scale.

A CORN LUNCHEON

By Eleanor M. Lucas

The table was covered with white damask, and for a centerpiece ears of corn formed an elongated enclosure. Perfect ears had been selected and the pale green husks had been drawn back and made to lie flat like the sepals of a flower, and from them rose the pearly ears of corn, standing upright, partly veiled in filmy corn silk. Arranged within and overrunning this enclosure were bright blue cornflowers and asparagus ferns. Both are so enduring that no water was required, so the greens and flowers were arranged in a loose mass, the greens trailing down the table toward either end, and, wherever they encountered a candlestick, wreathing themselves about it. The candlesticks stood in a row down the center of the table, two on each end, and were made from the long round boxes in which electric light mantles come, covered with corn husks; a drop of glue in the top of these made the blue candles secure. Little canoes, made of cardboard covered with corn husks, held the salted almonds and salted popped corn.

At each place was a wonderful corn-husk doll, bearing an armful of cornflowers, tied with pale creamy ribbons. On one end of the ribbon bow was written the guest's name and on the other the date. The menu was:

Cream of corn soup

Mock oysters   Sliced cucumbers

Lamb chops   Corn timbales
Mousseline sauce
Hot corn meal gems
Green pea and lettuce mayonnaise in corn-husk baskets
Cream cheese and olive sandwiches
Apricot sherbet in green jelly cups
Sponge cakes   Corn crisps
Coffee

A few of the dishes are given in detail:

Mock Oysters—To a cup of grated corn pulp, add a teaspoon of salt, a teaspoon of paprika and three well beaten eggs. Fry in butter, in small spoonfuls, dish on a napkin covered plate, garnish with parsley and lemon and serve with cucumbers.

Broil the chops and garnish with cress.

Corn Timbales—To one cup of grated corn pulp add one cup of milk, a teaspoon each of chopped parsley and onion juice, one soda cracker rolled fine and a teaspoon of salt. Beat two eggs until light, add to the other ingredients. Pour into buttered timbale molds, cook in a slow oven, the molds standing in a pan of hot water, until the centers are firm. Invert on a pretty dish, garnish with parsley and pour over each timbale a spoonful of sauce.

Mousseline Sauce—Beat a tablespoon of butter to a cream; add the yolks of three eggs, one at a time, then add three tablespoons of lemon juice, half a teaspoon of salt and a dash of cayenne. Cook over hot water until the sauce thickens, then add another tablespoon of butter and half a cup of sweet cream. When the sauce is hot, serve. It should be quite thick and frothy.

Hot Corn Meal Gems—Cream a tablespoon of butter and a tablespoon of sugar, add the yolks of two eggs and mix well. Place in the flour sifter one and a half cups each of white flour and corn meal, a teaspoon of salt and two teaspoons of baking powder. Add this gradually to the egg mixture with a cup and a half of sweet milk. Fold in lightly the stiffly-beaten whites of the eggs and pour into gem pans. Bake thirty minutes in a hot oven. This amount will make twenty-four small gems.

The timbales can be cooked some time in advance and reheated by standing in hot water, as the oven will be required for the gems.

Mayonnaise of Peas—Mix two cups of cooked chilled green peas with half a cup of thick mayonnaise. Make little square or oblong baskets of cardboard, cover with corn husks, a strip of cardboard covered with the husk serving as a handle. Fasten a few blue corn-flowers to one side and to the handle. Line with waxed paper, then with pale green lettuce leaves, allowing the leaves to come up above the sides. Fill with mayonnaise of peas, placing a spoonful of mayonnaise on top. This forms a pretty color effect.

Cheese and Olive Sandwiches—Beat the cream cheese until soft; to one small roll add six stoned olives chopped fine and a dash of cayenne. Spread on thin slices of buttered white bread and press together. Cut in small pieces and pile on a pretty lace paper doily.

Apricot Sherbet in Jelly Cups—Mix one pint of apricot pulp, the juice of two oranges and one lemon, the grated rind of the lemon and one pint of syrup (made by cooking for ten minutes two cups of sugar and one cup of water). Freeze in the usual way.

For the jelly cups, make a lemon jelly by softening one ounce of gelatine in one-third of a cup of cold water, add a pint of boiling water, stir until dissolved. Add a cup of sugar, and when cool the grated rind of a lemon, and the juice of four. Stir in enough spinach green to give a pretty green tint. Mold in little border molds or patent charlotte russe molds. When firm turn out and fill the hollow centers with the sherbet, which may be topped with a spoonful of whipped cream or sprinkled with a teaspoon of candied mint leaves.

Corn Crisps—Pop some corn and place in a large kettle. Boil one cup of molasses, one cup of sugar and half a cup of vinegar until it crisps when dropped into cold water. Pour this over two quarts of corn, measured after popping. Stir well with a long-handled spoon. When mixed pour into a shallow baking pan that has been lined with waxed paper. Press it down firmly, lay a piece of waxed paper on top and over this a board, smaller than the top of pan, so it will fit upon the mixture. On this place two or three flatirons. The next day remove the weight, board and paper, turn onto a clean board, remove paper from bottom and with a very sharp knife cut into slices. Lay these to dry, then wrap in waxed paper, or pile as they are on a pretty green plate.

EVE'S LUNCHEON

By Mary Dawson

Twenty-five Philadelphia girls were completely mystified by invitations bidding them to a "luncheon a l'Eve." It proved to be one of the most unique affairs of the season, everything being served as Eve would have offered it in Eden, that is without knife, fork or spoon. An entire menu which could be daintily conveyed to the mouth with the hands would have sounded like an utter impossibility until our hostess showed us the way to do it. Afterward, like Columbus' egg, it was the simplest thing in the world. Oysters were out of season, and out of the question, too, but fruit was seasonable and dainty to handle, accordingly the first course was fruit. Each plate contained a small bunch of grapes, a couple of ripe plums, portions of bananas having the skin curled down to protect the fingers, and various other tidbits that were certain not to prove too juicy. The soup, too, was easy when one knew how. It came to table in small china cups with handles. The toast squares that accompanied this course were chosen because less likely to crumble than bread.

One of the courses was meat patties in little fluted cases of pastry. These were so tiny and so crisp that they could be eaten without forks. The lamb chops that followed were also very small. They were fitted out with white curled papers at the bone end so that not a finger was soiled in handling them. Saratoga chips, lettuce, cress and corn on the cob were the green things of the feast. We curled the white lettuce leaves into little bunches, as the French epicures do, and dipped them into a creamy mayonnaise. The butter problem was disposed of by bread and butter sandwiches cut very thin and rolled, and by hot wheat muffins split and buttered before being brought to the table. For dessert we had a frappe served in cups with handles, wee tartlets filled with compote of fresh fruit, cakes, candies, coffee, salted nuts and other good things.

A CHINESE LUNCHEON

Which Can Be Followed or Adapted by College Girls and Other Girls

Chrysanthemums, cherry blossoms, chopsticks, chow ming, chop suey and everything Chinese was the order at a charming luncheon given by a young woman. She did not plan the table nor prepare the luncheon herself; she engaged the chef of a Chinese restaurant and his corps of waiters to carry out the affair, while she herself, having sojourned in China and owning a fine collection of Chinese curiosities, overlooked the picturesque part of the entertainment and made use of every possibility. The hostess waited to receive in a Chinese coat of tawny silk with splendid embroideries. The dining room was a complete transformation scene. From Chinese lanterns was shed a subdued light. The room was hung with a frieze of painted silk decorated with Chinese landscapes where delicate-footed Chinese ladies were seen picking their way through a world which seemed all moonshine. There were showers of chrysanthemums over yards and yards of the strange moonshiny silk on which a Chinese artist loves to trail his dreamy fancies. In odd contrast to the moonshine were the red and yellow Chinese flags and splendid splashes of oriental coloring. It glowed in massive urns and vases, in richly decorated jars and magnificent screens. The mantel was draped with Chinese silk and yards of rich embroideries trailed over the chair backs.

The table as set for a Chinese luncheon was perhaps the most interesting thing in the room. It was shadowed by an enormous Japanese umbrella, around which hung lanterns. The table was a bare mahogany, but drifted everywhere among the dishes were tiny white Chinese lilies, not unlike orchids and as fragrant as freesias. There was no grouping of dishes such as American taste demands. The small plates of sweetmeats and nuts, which take the place of our olives and relishes, were arranged together in geometrical forms, in open squares and stiff triangles. Each plate held a certain number of sweetmeats, pomegranates or nuts, three, five, seven or nine, set also in geometrical primness. At each cover was one pair of chopsticks, a droll china ladle, two teacups, a tiny dish of soy and a napkin, which was changed at each of the eleven courses. It was not easy at first to eat soup from a ladle or meat from a pair of chopsticks, but before the end of the luncheon each guest was an expert in the art and would not have quailed at the prospect of appearing at a Chinese legation luncheon.

The first thing served was gue sine tea, in bits of tiny, dragon-decorated china with handles like our bouillon cups. After the tea came Chinese preserves, candied fruits and sweetmeats, although of indescribable flavor. Cam ghet, ton guhg, bor low and lichee nuts were the relishes of most intelligible name. Bor low gay, famous bird's nest soup, followed the sweetmeats. It was served with a delicate garnishing of shredded chicken and eaten from china ladles. Again came chicken, fried and boneless, with fresh mushrooms and water nuts as an accompaniment. The *piece de resistance* of the feast was roasted duck, buried in a snowy mound of chrysanthemum petals. Chop suey was the next course; then came yocklumine, a delicious combination of fish, tender bamboo sprouts, shredded ham, mushrooms and water nuts. One triumphant dish, on which a Chinese cook prides himself as sure to please the American, is lobster omelet, and on this occasion the chef was besieged for the recipe. A Chinese chef, however, rarely condescends to bestow such a favor; he looks delightfully blank, forgets his English utterly and smiles a benign gentle smile. Rice cooked Chinese fashion is scarcely recognizable as the same thing we often find in a moist mush on our tables. At such a feast as the one described, rice never appears; it would be scorned as too plebeian; but by the entreaty of the hostess, it followed the omelet. Then came chow ming, a fried noodle with meat, which was that last substantial course. The dessert was China cakes, delicious though of strange seasoning, and Chinese toasted almonds.

The ladies adjourned with the clearing away of dessert to a tea bench in a corner of the dining room, a table surrounded by a bench at which the last tea drinking of a meal is always held in a Chinese home. Around the bare board the ladies drank soung soe tea.

All the circumstance and form attendant on a meal eaten chopstick fashion was carried out during the luncheon. The hostess in the apparel of a Chinese lady acted as a real Chinese dame would have done in her place. With the appearance of a new course on the table, she praised each dish in the most extravagant fashion. The guests agreed, with a lavishness of admiring flattery. The meal was eaten with thin blue clouds of delicate incense wreathing themselves about the room. It was burned, as it always is at a Chinese feast, in a splendid brass bowl. There were no individual finger bowls. When the party rose from the table they followed their hostess to a great china bowl on a teakwood table set against a magnificent screen. It held perfumed water, into which each lady dipped her fingers.

The following out of such a luncheon as this by a hostess who could not engage a Chinese chef and a corps of silk gowned waiters, is not an impossibility. It would require something of originality, a faculty for adapting ideas, not a little research of Chinese customs and dishes, and a tactful choice of one's guests, for half the success of an affair of this sort would depend on the bright, intelligent women invited to participate.

EASTER LUNCHEONS

A pleasing feature of all Eastertide entertainments is the profuse use of flowers and decorations of green, which suggest the spring. Of the almost innumerable functions which can be given, the three following are suggested:

The breakfast is the simplest form, and differs from the luncheon only in that the hour is earlier, usually 12 o'clock; and the menu is less elaborate. Both the breakfast and luncheon are well adapted to a dozen or fewer guests. A basket filled with primroses of the various delicate colors tied with a ribbon of pale green makes a beautiful and springlike centerpiece. The menu should contain as many fresh fruits and vegetables as possible, and the whole affair should be as expressive of the spring as it can be made.

BREAKFAST MENU

Grape fruit and Malaga grapes

Puree of spinach

Bread sticks

Lobster cutlets

Cucumber jelly   Rolls

Sweetbread fillets, maitre d'hotel sauce

Potato roses   Asparagus tips

Tomato aspic and celery salad

Sandwiches   Camembert cheese   Olives

Toasted water biscuit

Coffee   Salted nuts   Candies

The combination of grape fruit and Malaga grapes is delicious. The grape fruit is cut in half and prepared as usual, only that the grapes, skinned and seeded, are mixed with it. A brandied cherry is placed on top. These are prettier served on maidenhair ferns than on doilies.

The puree of spinach is a delicate green, served with a little whipped cream on top, but not enough entirely to cover it. The lobster cutlets may be garnished with parsley, and the cucumber jelly made a little greener with leaf green. The cucumber jelly is served in individual forms with a few pieces of the cucumber in the top. The asparagus tips are served with drawn butter sauce and the potato roses are made with a pastry bag. The tomato aspic is made in a ring mold and the center is filled with celery salad mayonnaise. This makes a pretty bit of color, as well as being crisp and refreshing. Lettuce sandwiches are a good combination with this salad. The omission of a sweet simplifies the breakfast. The Camembert cheese served with hot toasted water biscuit is followed by the demitasse of coffee.

The same number of people may be more elaborately entertained at a luncheon. Too many flowers cannot be used to make the occasion attractive, but the simplest table decorations are always the prettiest. A low centerpiece is the best form. Baskets, tied with large bows of ribbon, are very much used, but a foundation of asparagus or maidenhair ferns or galax leaves is very effective with any of the spring flowers; the delicate

A LUNCHEON TABLE

pink tulips make a beautiful centerpiece with the ferns. A variety of flowers may be used by placing at each plate a bunch of a different kind, as lilacs, jonquils, narcissus, lilies of the valley, sweet peas, California violets, crocus, hyacinths and mignonette; or they may be tied to the backs of the chairs with pale pink ribbons. This makes the dining room look like a mass of flowers as the guests enter. A simple and individual place card has only one's crest or monogram done in gold.

LUNCHEON MENU

Strawberries on green leaves
Cold bouillon, crouton sticks
Cold lobster, mayonnaise
Cheese souffle in green peppers
Sandwiches
Beef mignons broiled, mushroom sauce
Potato timbales   Peas
Garcia salad   Cheese crackers
Ice cream fruit forms on maidenhair ferns
Glace cakes
Marrons   Fig paste   Salted nuts
Coffee

If strawberries are used, five good sized ones are enough for each person, served on the green leaves, or if unattainable, on ferns, with powdered sugar on the plate in small paper cases. Another fruit or fruit salad can be substituted if the berries are too expensive or not to be had.

The crouton sticks served with the cold bouillon are made as follows: Cut bread into one-fourth-inch slices, remove crusts, spread slightly with butter on both sides, cut into strips one-fourth inch wide, bake until light brown. If the bouillon will not become firm enough of itself, a little pulverized gelatine can be used; it is just as delicate this way. One-half of a small cold boiled lobster served with a very heavy mayonnaise is the fish course. The entree may be the cheese souffle baked in green peppers, or an egg course is always in place here.

To make the layers, cut several slices of brown and white bread one-fourth inch, butter each, then put five together, alternating them. Cut down in slices one-fourth inch thick. This gives a sandwich of three brown and two white strips. The beef mignons are tenderloins cut three-fourths inch thick. If these are not to be had, substitute fillet of beef. Fresh mushrooms would add very much to this course, but they are beyond the average purse.

Garcia Salad—Cut celery, apples, and fresh tomatoes in thin strips about two inches long, serve on lettuce leaves with French dressing. A slice of truffle on the top adds both to the appearance and flavor.

Serve the crackers hot with melted cheese on top. Nothing in ices is prettier than the beautifully colored fruit forms served on maidenhair ferns in a large silver dish. Small squares of homemade cakes can be substituted for the glace cakes if desired. The coffee is served in the drawing room.

The third form of entertainment is a buffet luncheon at which from twenty-five to one hundred and fifty guests can be entertained. It is more elaborate than a reception and less general. The guests are all invited for the same hour, usually 2 o'clock. The luncheon can be served in three ways. The guests may fill the dining room and be served as at a reception; or by having chairs enough to seat all the guests at one time scattered about through the various rooms. In this case a pretty feature is to have a small table set (with cloth or doilies, bonbons, etc.) in the center of each room with one or two matrons to pour the coffee and chocolate. Each table can have a different color in flowers and candles, to correspond with those of the room. Or, with a limited number of guests, small tables, each seating four or six, can be set out through all the rooms. Four courses are the usual number, though more may be served when all are seated at tables, the form being bouillon, fish, croquettes, salad and sandwiches and a sweet; also coffee and chocolate. The fish course may be omitted and lobster Newburg be served with the croquette, the salad served as a separate course. If the guests are few enough in number to be served at small tables, and a more elaborate menu is desired, the following can be used: Caviar, bouillon, fish, croquettes and peas, salad and a sweet, coffee, chocolate.

TEN-CENT LUNCHEONS

By C. A. L.

A number of good and enthusiastic housekeepers, realizing how far from ideal the present methods of

OF GREEN BURLAP, WITH CHINESE COINS

living are, how unrefreshing and how conventional, "planned a plan," namely, a scheme for serving practicable luncheons at ten cents a plate. In order to have some fun out of their experiments, they planned to share the luncheons, each one in turn acting as both cook and hostess to the other eleven.

The third of these object lessons was given recently. The table, set for twelve in a room where gay lights were substituted for sunlight, was polished so highly that all the ware and decorations were reflected in its mahogany depths. Fruits and vegetables in season made a decoration which was rich and harmonious in coloring. The hostess, too busy with her menu to receive her guests, turned that pleasure over to a friend, and when she appeared at table, it was in "cookie's" garb of starchy white and a captivating baker's cap.

The menu for the luncheon was done on green burlap ornamented with ten pennies. On one side the simple dishes were enumerated in French phraseology. On the reverse side appeared the voucher for the cost of the materials which went into the feast—everything— bread, butter, potatoes, crackers, etc. Translated, the appetizing menu read:

Julienne soup in cups

Hot French bread   Butter balls

Fish au gratin with potatoes in their jackets

Beans and lettuce salad

Rabbit stew

Piece de resistance

Timbales of spinach and small peas

Dessert

Strawberry cakes with charlotte russe
Wafers   California cheese
Black coffee

Hors d'oeuvre

Olives

Chef d'oeuvre

Surprise salad for the refreshment of the spirit

It was over the cook's "work of art" that the company lingered and made merry. It was a tempting dish of salad made of realistic green-yellow paper leaves within which was hidden the following guessing game:

1. A large European city and green. 2. Green and a dairy product. 3. Green and a portion of the human anatomy. 4. Green and a musical instrument. 5. Green and a reptile. 6. Green and a dwelling. 7. A synonym for always and green. 8. Green and a common name for material. 9. Green and a portion of a house. 10. Green, an elevation of land and a part of the United States. 11. Green and part of the earth's surface.

The key to the game may be passed by, if the reader wishes to guess the blanks himself. These are the answers: 1, Paris green; 2, green cheese; 3, greenback; 4, greenhorn; 5, green turtle; 6, greenhouse; 7, evergreen; 8, green goods; 9, greenroom; 10, Green Mountain state; 11, Greenland. The first prize was a

THE HOSTESS OF THE TEN-CENT LUNCHEON

lettuce leaf plate of majolica, the consolation, a head
of lettuce.

The two luncheons which were given previous to
this one would be found equally original and interesting
and were also most successful, yet not one hostess but
will tell you that it is not at all the impossible which
she is attempting, even though she must weigh and
measure and even cut that she may accomplish the
desired end. And besides the fact of having given and
received much simple pleasure, the hostesses of the ten-
cent luncheons have found that buying with so much
thought and care brings with it the knowledge of many
unsuspected possibilities in the household economy.

A MAY TIME LUNCHEON

By Marjorie March

In giving a luncheon two things are of prime
importance: daintiness of service, congeniality of guests.
The latter requirement is, of course, true at any entertainment, but more especially at a formal luncheon
or dinner, where the life of success must depend upon
conversation. As we have the wealth of May's bounty
at our command let us choose either apple blooms, dog-
wood or the wild azalea as the floral decoration, and as
fashion has given us our choice of serving luncheon
either at one central table or at several little ones,
let us by all means choose the small tables. These
should be covered with small white cloths. A vase of
flowers in the center of each, say, shall we, of apple

blossoms. The china, if possible, should be pink and white in such a case, and everything that can be pink should lend its support to the color scheme. In the center of the room place a table from which the waitresses serve the accessories of the luncheon. Those things such as cakes, candies, fruits, etc., which are ornamental as well as useful, can be made be utiful for the eye to delight in. An enormous bushel basket, given a rough coat of white enamel paint and tied about with one or two bands of pink ribbon four or five inches in width—a big bow with flying ends at the side where it is tied—should stand in the center. In this basket some vessel, which of course is entirely concealed, should hold a generous supply of water to give life and freshness to the huge bouquet of pink and white apple blossoms which is the burden the basket is to bear. Trailing over the table cover in careless, wandering style, smilax should trace its course, falling over the edge of the table and caught here and there by little butterfly-like bows of pink ribbon. Silver bonbon dishes set here and there amid the smilax should hold pink candies, etc. The vases of apple blossoms on the smaller tables can have their bouquets tied with pink ribbon if desired, but this is not necessary.

The menu might be as follows: Grape fruit served with sherry and candied cherries; creamed sweetbreads in pink paper cases; chicken croquettes, Saratoga chips and cranberry jelly sandwiches; egg salad, served on lettuce leaves, the yolks of the eggs being colored pink; pink ices and fancy cakes; fruits and candy.

A CURIOSITY TEA

By Mary Dawson

My first acquaintance with this amusing little entertainment was made about two weeks ago. It proved to be exceedingly good fun. The invitations, which were written on note paper odd in shape and color, had a postscript which read: "Please come bringing a curiosity with you." At first I thought I should merely take the invitation note sheet, for that seemed to me to be quite curiosity enough. But on thinking it over I left the note at home and took as my contribution a "freak" photograph, the result of peculiar atmospheric conditions. Each "invitee" came bringing some curiosity, as the notes requested. The hostess as she greeted each arrival requested him or her not to reveal the secret of the curiosity brought to other players; that is, what it was or how formed. The curiosities as they came were arranged upon a large table. A card with a number was attached to each exhibit. They made an odd looking collection, in which heirlooms, botanical freaks, eccentricities from India and China, et cetera, figured. When all the guests had arrived we were given pencils and note books and asked to write the nature and history of each object as nearly as we could guess them. Everyone enjoyed the nonsense of this guessing, especially as nobody was permitted to help any other contestant. The hostess had in hand two odd little articles which were found in a foreign shop in New York as prizes. These

A BROWN BETTY TEAPOT

were awarded for the first and second best list of answers. A table was arranged as for an ordinary tea in the dining room. When the guessing was over we were duly refreshed with salads and sandwiches, ice cream, cake, coffee and the like.

THE SPINSTER'S TEA

By T. C. C.

A bevy of girls of our town, with the aid of an older head, planned a very enjoyable evening. The invitations were headed with a clever pen and ink sketch of a cat, the "spinster's solace." We invited the guests to come at 3 o'clock in the afternoon and to appear in the costume of the traditional spinster of "ye olden time." The majority of the girls wore corkscrew curls and all of them old-time gowns. They carried reticules and quaint bead bags containing sprigs of fennel, sweet flagroot and peppermint drops. Each one told a story of her courtship and why her lover was rejected. The guest telling the best story received as a prize a fine picture of a cat. After that we had a guessing match, the contestant giving the greatest number of correct answers to a series of cat questions being awarded the prize—a black cat pin cushion. The questions and answers were as follows: Library cat, catalog; aspiring cat, catamount; tree cat, catalpa; near relation, catkin; water cat, cataract; dangerous cat, catastrophe; barber cat, polecat; spicy cat, catsup; cat's favorite plant, catnip; musical cat, catgut. We had photographs taken at the conclusion of the tea. This was served at 5 o'clock. The table was a long, old-fashioned one of mahogany, and all the quaint china and glassware obtainable was used on it. The menu included old-fashioned viands and preserves, cookies, hot biscuit, cold chicken, rich fruit cake, gold and silver cake, and other old-time varieties. Daguerreotypes, miniatures and faded photographs of relatives were brought by most of the "spinsters," and there was lots of fun inspecting them. After the tea we sang Auld Lang Syne and other ballads of "ye olden time."

A SOFA PILLOW TEA

A sewing circle for young girls realized one hundred dollars for a charitable object by a novel entertainment which they christened a sofa pillow tea. The first twenty-five meetings of the circle had been devoted to the production of sofa pillows only, with a result of a hundred smart cushions. The invitations for the tea had the words "pillow sale" written in the lower left-hand corner, a hint for the charitably inclined to bring their purses. A little reception alcove on one side of the hall had been fitted up for displaying the cushions, which were arranged upon a couple of large tables. Each had a neat ticket giving materials used and price. After greeting the hostess and meeting friends the guests wandered through to the cushion room. Refreshments were served in the dining room.

PARTIES FOR CHILDREN

PARTIES FOR CHILDREN

A HAPPY CHRISTENING

By Leila Lyon Topping

ONE sunshiny spring day the little autocrat came into his own—silently, gravely, with a dignity befitting a ruler of many hearts, and after that his serene majesty was known as Richard the Second. Some of the guests who were present that day have never forgotten the little group in the vine-hung bay window of the pretty drawing room. The pale, slant rays of the setting sun fell upon the rector's silvery locks, touched the earnest face of the father, and rested halo-wise above the pure face of the young mother, down bent upon the lovely wondering babe in her arms.

There was a charming simplicity about it all: the baby's gown, exquisitely plain, but of a gossamer sheerness, the mother herself in a severely simple white frock, whose chastely flowing lines were a fit setting for the gracious, Madonna-like curves of its wearer. A small Flemish oak table, covered with a square of point lace, held the baptismal bowl of heavy antique silver, the party stood on a white fur rug, and there was a white satin kneeling pillow. Glass bowls of white hyacinths and roses were scattered about the room, and there were plenty of candles, but these were not lighted until after the ceremony.

AN ALPHABET SET

A NURSERY RHYME SET

When the guests had paid obeisance to the little king, and he had departed to the upper regions, a simple tea was informally served in the pretty dining room. On the way thither, everyone dropped in at the library to see the gifts, which were attractively displayed upon a table covered with a white satin spread embroidered with flying storks in blue. A many-branching silver candelabrum in the center shed a soft glow upon the dainty gifts, which were of every conceivable sort.

The tea table looked very attractive and the decorations were especially suggestive and appropriate. A silver cradle filled with hyacinths and lilies of the valley rested on a square of point lace over white satin. This was bordered with small white paper moccasins, each one holding a growing fern of some dwarf variety and a tiny white candle; there were eight on a side and they made a brave showing when lighted. Two pretty girls presided over the punch bowl and samovar at opposite sides of the table, and several others helped to serve the guests, no servants appearing. From the steaming samovar came delicious tea served in tall glasses, and the punch bowl held a fragrant fruit punch, the base of which was lemonade, from which shredded pineapple, orange and banana had been strained, with Maraschino cherries added.

There were molds of jellied chicken, with salad sandwiches, rolled and tied with white ribbons, and there were also sweet sandwiches of various sorts. These were cut heart shaped and filled, some with peach or orange marmalade, chopped pineapple and cream cheese, and still others were made of graham bread spread with raisins and chopped English walnuts.

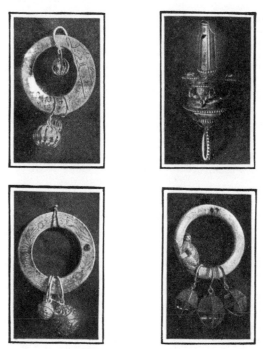

GIFTS FOR THE BABY

A pleasing novelty were the ice cream sandwiches. The little cakes and bonbons were all white and green, and there were pistache nuts sprinkled among the salted pecans, with several dishes of crystallized fruits, pineapple, orange and angelica. Everything was prepared at home and was dainty and successful to a degree of perfection. The salad sandwiches, which were especially delectable, were made of chicken, pounded to a paste and mixed with a green mayonnaise, then spread between crisp lettuce leaves, and all the sweet fillings were bound together with whipped cream.

The ice cream sandwiches are delightful and easily made, provided that the cream—in bricks, of course—be very firm and cut upon a marble slab with a cake cutter. Pineapple cream was used between champagne wafers, and pistache with macaroons, on this occasion, the color scheme being consistently carried out in every detail.

A PAPER PARTY

By Virginia Van De Water

The invitations for this party should be issued long enough beforehand for the parents of the children to prepare for them costumes of tissue paper. This will not be found so difficult as it sounds. Any woman who is deft with her fingers can make such a costume for her small boy or girl. If possible, let her visit one of the fashion plate shops where are displayed the latest models of gowns done in tissue paper, and she will soon see what really pretty effects can be produced. The mother of each guest may send word to the hostess what color her costume will be and the hostess will then get a fancy paper cap to match each dress and suit.

The parlors and hall and dining room can be decorated with Chinese lanterns and tissue paper flowers and streamers. Over the dining table may be hung a huge paper umbrella of the Japanese variety and from the tip of each rib of this is suspended a paper bag containing some trifle such as a tiny Chinese doll, or a Chinese pig, or any one of the many favors that can be bought at an oriental shop. The table is spread with a white cloth, and lighted by candles with colored paper shades. Refreshments are served in papier mache plates. Japanese paper napkins are at each place.

When the little ones are assembled all are told to hunt for the caps that match their costume. These caps are hidden about the rooms, and each child is instructed not to touch any cap except one that is of the same color as his clothes. This gives rise to a great deal of merriment, for the boy or girl who carelessly or rashly puts the tip of a finger on a cap of any hue save the one belonging to him or her is required to pay a forfeit, and after the head coverings are all found a game of forfeit follows.

Then provide each child with a pair of scissors, a pencil, and a sheet of paper. Each names some animal he or she will first draw, then cut out. The one making the best picture wins a prize, the one making the funniest receives a booby prize. The first prize for the girls may be a pretty paper doll with her wardrobe, that can be put on and off. The first prize for the boys is a handsome paper-covered book. The booby prize for the girls can be a tiny fan, for the boys a small grotesque Japanese doll. After the prizes are distributed each child takes his place in the middle of the group and tells what animal he has attempted to draw, while the circle of children make the noise natural to the animal named.

The refreshments are now served to the children at the large dining table, or carried into the drawing room to them, where they may be seated about in groups. Serve iced bouillon, chicken sandwiches, thin slices of tongue, ices, cakes and lemonade. Each child has given him a little paper box of candy that had been put at his place at the supper table and this he takes home with him.

When the refreshments are eaten, clear the dining table, and move away the chairs. Stand the children in a row around the board, and hand to each in order a long stiff switch or stick; or you may give the switches to all at once. With these the little ones are to hook the bags off the tips of the umbrella ribs. It will require a little care to slip the end of the stick through the loop of string by which the paper bag is suspended and lift it down without dropping it. Fortunately, the contents of the parcels are of the unbreakable variety, so no damage is done if they fall.

If there is any time left before the hour for departure, have some comparatively quiet games such as "ring around a rosy," or "hunt the slipper," always bearing in mind that paper costumes, while pretty and effective, are not proof against the rough handling inseparable from romping games.

A WINTER PICNIC

By Hester Price

Margie Dean was a little girl who had been patient and good through a long illness, but now that she felt strong again it seemed hard to her that she could not run and play with the boys and girls she knew. One day she was standing at the window mournfully watching the children go by with their sleds and skates, when her mother said: "Margie, let's have your little friends spend Saturday here. Suppose we play 'tis summer and ask all the boys and girls to a winter picnic."

The invitations were short notes on small sheets of white paper with a bit of fern at the top of each. You may imagine the children's surprise when they read: "Will you come down to my pond at 1 o'clock Saturday?" They asked each other: "Did your note have 125 Blank street on it? How can Margie Dean have a pond in the house? Where does she keep it?" You may be sure they all decided not to go skating that Saturday.

What fun Margie and her mother had getting ready! They moved all the potted plants to the dining room. They covered the sideboard, serving table and mantelpiece with white. Here and there they scattered a few ferns and Margie arranged some cat-tails she had brought from the country last summer in a great jar in one corner.

MARGIE'S POND

The round table was covered with denim of a soft green. In the center of the table was the pond. This pond was really a round mirror with edges concealed with smilax. On its surface were toy ducks and geese, little toys of the most inexpensive sort, while grazing on the banks were miniature cows, horses and sheep. The chandelier was entirely concealed with branches of arbor vitae. Over the tablecloth were scattered a few ferns and white narcissi.

The menu was very simple, but each course was so "picnicky" that the children entered merrily into the fun. This was what they had for the picnic luncheon:

Malaga grapes
Bouillon
Thin bread and butter
Broiled chicken   Potato straws
Brown bread and butter
Sandwiches   Cocoa
Cream cheese and lettuce
Nut sandwiches
Bird's nest pudding.   Whipped cream
Small cakes

The fruit course was in place when the children entered the dining room. Though very simply arranged this added greatly to the charm of the table. Mrs. Dean had made small nests of excelsior and placed one at each cover filled with Malaga grapes. Under each nest was a fern frond. After the first course small packages, wrapped in Japanese napkins and tied with yellow and green baby ribbon, were passed. These packages proved to be sandwiches made of different things and to be eaten with the different courses.

The potato straws were crisp and dry. With each cup of cocoa were two papier mache straws. The cream cheese was made into small "bird's eggs," flecked with pepper and disposed in nests of lettuce. The blancmange was molded in eggshells that Margie had taken great delight in "blowing." They were arranged upon a flat platter in a nest of whipped cream. For this course spoons were passed, and Margie gaily reminded her friends that even at an outdoor picnic one spoon was allowed and she had saved them for the whipped cream. The small cakes were iced in three tints, white, yellow and pale green.

At the very last a tray was passed, piled high with round bags of yellow and green crepe paper. These bags were simply squares of crepe paper fluffed at the edges, filled with marshmallows and tied with baby ribbon. The spring colors made a pretty showing and the opening of the packages was an added pleasure for the children.

When the picnic was over Mrs. Dean gathered the children around a big wood fire and beguiled them into discussing summer days, gardening, and the flowers they loved best. Together they went through flower catalogs till their enthusiasm was high. She then left the room and when she came back she had a pretty bag filled with small packages of flower seeds. From this each child was allowed to take a package and she told them to wait until spring and then plant the seed and see what flowers would grow.

The recipes used for the luncheon were the following:

Potato Straws—Potato straws are light and harmless and should not be classed with harmful fried food. Cut the straws lengthwise of the potato, first in slices about one-eighth of an inch thick, and then into straws the length of the slices. They should be cooked quickly in hot fat until crisp and of a lemon color. The straws are especially pretty if cut with a fluted knife.

Nut Sandwiches—Cut thin slices of buttered graham bread into circles with a small biscuit cutter. Place on top of each sandwich the meat of one-half of an English walnut. The walnuts may be held in place with a little butter.

Bird's Nest Pudding—Put one pint of milk on to heat in a double boiler, moisten four tablespoons of cornstarch mixed with four tablespoons sugar with a little cold milk and stir into the hot milk; stir until it thickens, then add a teaspoon of vanilla. Have ready some eggshells that have been emptied from a small hole in the top, fill them with this mixture, stand them in a pan of Indian meal or flour to prevent them from falling over, and put in a cold place to harden. Whip a pint of cream, dispose the cornstarch eggs upon a round platter, surrounded with a nest of whipped cream.

FOR THE LITTLE FOLKS

By B. P.

I know of no expenditure of time and work which yields such a return in pleasure as entertaining a party of children. "It blesses him that gives and him that takes," except in cases where the latter is in danger of being killed by excess of culinary kindness. I have observed, too, that children are just as contented, and far happier as to their insides, if quantity and quality instead of bewildering variety, be kept in mind in providing the table. It is most important that the dishes served be those easily assimilated and easily digested together. An unwise selection of things, each good by itself alone, has sent many a little tot home to have a "pain under his apron" or rather under his nightie (as I believe all children take darkness and the "wee sma' hours" to enjoy this common affliction at its best). I feel it is such a pity to give rich and conflicting food to children!

Among the many desirable and reasonably safe items from which a suitable menu may be selected are the following: any form of bouillon or cream soup in cups; nourishing sandwiches or tiny buttered rolls, with cold meats sliced thin—tongue (not canned) and turkey or chicken. As a rule, children prefer the last to all meats, so either creamed or cold it always disappears in astonishing quantities, and when creamed, peas are good with it. Novel and ornamental small cakes, cookies or kisses; custards, junkets or a simple homemade ice cream; and pure candy—the ribbon candies which look so much and amount to so little. For drinks, chocolate is particularly attractive to young people, with its white cap of whipped cream; lemonade (sometimes), and plenty of water. Ice cream may be molded in forms and enjoyed with the eyes, but is too often so hard that it is no pleasure to eat it, and I think it better to have softer cream served in small fancy cases. Fresh or canned pineapple is a wholesome accompaniment, as this fruit contains an acid which helps to digest milk. But, do your best, and once in a while one comes across a freaky child who is not satisfied with anything on the table. I well remember our efforts to warm and fill one bashful guest—scarcely more than a baby—who after refusing everything, timidly raised his serious brown eyes and asked if we had any cold potatoes in the house! I give a recipe for a nutritious broth which makes a good beginning for little and big:

Three pounds of beef cut from the shin; three pounds of bone from same, cracked; four quarts of water, and four teaspoons of salt. Trim off the dried skin and other unusable parts of the meat, cut the remainder into small pieces, place with the other ingredients in a covered earthen jar and let stand one hour before setting in a slow oven to cook from eight to twelve hours. Put through a coarse strainer and when cold remove fat. In serving, add more seasoning if you wish, and never heat above one hundred and seventy-five degrees. This may also be used as a jelly.

A plate of little turtle cakes never fails to call
forth squeals of delight. Bake a plain cake mixture in
tiny pans in a hot oven; frost and put a fat raisin in
the center of each before the frosting hardens; pinch the
buds out of four small cloves and arrange for feet; use
one, containing the bud, for a head; and the pointed
stem of another for a tail. Plain cookies, cut in shapes
of oak or maple leaves and frosted with green frosting,
are both delicious and wholesome; and cookies sugared
and bearing the initials of the guests in white frosting;
or frosted first and the letters put on with an icing colored with chocolate, are far more tempting than cookies
that are less individual.

For a birthday, the crowning glory of the table is
the cake, resplendent with candles. The candles are
lighted and allowed to burn during the eating of the
refreshments, each child blowing out one of the lights
just before cutting the cake, which is passed round last
of all. Mothers are few who can refuse this pleasure,
but one who had an abnormal fear of fire compromised
by allowing a single huge wax candle to burn in the
center of the cake, using as a safe holder the cylindrical
opening left by the tube pan in the baking. The cake
should be of good size and plain in every way save
looks. The good old fashion of inserting in the dough
when in the pan a silver thimble, a ring, a new ten-
cent piece and a bean, never loses its charm. When the
cake is cut there is always excitement till the one who
is to be first married gets the ring (and I have known
young women of four years to be intensely interested in

this superstition); whoever gets the bean will be a ruler, nothing *less* than president, probably; the thimble denotes an ideal housewife, in embryo; and she who gets the silver piece will have riches all her days. In olden times, when sensibilities were perhaps not so acute, somebody found a clove in the cake, and so proclaimed himself a knave-to-be.

Do not use confectioner's sugar to frost the cake, but white of egg and pulverized sugar or a boiled icing. Sprinkle with grated cocoanut and ornament the top with a border of tiny chocolate drops or candied cherries, or with crystallized fruit cut into bits, or with candied caraway seeds. Dainty candle holders in all colors are for sale at confectioners', but a pretty substitute can be made of a fringe of tissue paper wound tightly around each candle before setting into the frosting; spread out the fringe to catch any wax.

At the last party at which I officiated, the candles were so numerous that we cut a ring of pasteboard—its inside diameter being just that of the cake at the base— covered it with green tissue paper and ornamented it with laurel leaves. On this frame yellow candles were fixed. The table was trimmed with sprays and branches of laurel, with tangerine oranges invisibly tied to them to simulate the natural growth of the fruit. These made an effective showing and precious souvenirs to carry home.

If candles are not to be used, a cake which is a favorite with owners of a sweet tooth is one made of an angel cake mixture, baked in two parts and put

From a Photograph by Helen West Cooke

A VERY IMPORTANT BIRTHDAY PARTY, WITH JUST ONE CANDLE

together with a layer of marshmallows which have been soaked a short time in milk strongly flavored with sherry. The top is to be covered with the same and garnished profusely with whipped cream—also flavored with sherry—and put on with a star pastry tube. The cake and the cream need very little sugar.

The making of popcorn balls always pleases little people, the greater part of the corn being popped beforehand, of course; and a wonder-ball party, while a more serious undertaking, is sure to make a hit. Bits of presents are bought or made—charms, money, doll's gear and what-not—and one used as the center of a ball of worsted, which, as it is wound, conceals the little gifts wrapped in soft paper and put in from time to time. The receiver begins to knit on coarse needles, and as the yarn is used the little surprises fall out. It is certainly a great incentive to industry to have something nice drop into your lap while you work; but it needs a very patient mother and assistants to look out for dropped stitches.

For girls of a little older growth, the idea of an entertainment designated in the invitation sent my small niece of twelve as "a blissful tea," deserves to be passed along. After greeting her hostess, each guest is given a menu card, with pencil attached, upon which are numbers, from one to ten or more, with a blank space after each; and across the top the line, "Where ignorance is bliss," in gold lettering. A colored reproduction of some dainty dish, cut from advertisements, is pasted neatly on each card, the things in the bill of fare being suggested so far as possible. (These cards were manufactured by the little girl who gave the party, and that is where part of her fun came in.) The recipient writes her name on the card, puts a check mark against the numbers she selects and the orders are duly served by friends in caps and aprons, who fill them from another room after consulting a similar card which has the list completed and tacked up over the serving table; for example:

1. Glass of child's punch.
2. Chicken croquette.
3. College ice.
4. Cup of chocolate.
5. Olive.
6. Box of candy.
7. Toothpick.
8. Rolled sandwiches.
9. Glass of water.
10. Macaroons

The numbers may be increased, or other articles readily substituted for the ones on this list. The first order may be limited to five or six numbers, and a second order to two, to provide for a supposable case when an unfortunate has checked perhaps, one, five, six, seven and nine, and finds that ignorance is neither blissful nor filling. A supply of small tables set in convenient spots is a necessity for a party of this kind.

Child's Punch—Boil together for five minutes one quart of water and one and one-half pounds of sugar;

add grated rind of one lemon and one orange, and when cool, strain. Add juice of two oranges and four lemons. Pour in a pitcher with a lump of ice, add a quarter of a pound each of candied cherries and pineapple cut fine, and a quart of water.

Peanut Cream—Three pints of peanuts, shelled and put through a chopper adjusted to cut as fine as possible, two cups of sugar, two-thirds of a cup of milk and a small piece of butter. Stir together till dissolved the sugar, butter and milk; then cook without disturbing till it spins a thread, or till you can make a soft ball of a little of the syrup dropped in ice water. Take from the fire and while one person stirs, another must pour in the nuts. Beat till thick and creamy, pour into buttered pans and cut in small squares when cold.

The amusing experiment of a Lilliputian naval battle—which is so old that I trust it is new—always entertains a company of boys. Let them model, say, a dozen or more pieces of chalk to resemble ships, making the bottoms even, and using matches (without tips) for masts, smokestacks and turrets. Color part of them with black ink and leave the rest white. Put the different colors—the opposing forces—in a row along the sides of a very large platter and draw an imaginary line lengthwise across it. Let each boy choose sides, and then let the lord high admiral (the young host) carefully pour a good quantity of vinegar between the chalk sticks. Instantly there will be an audible seething, like the hissing of shells in actual warfare, while the ships will begin to move forward in slow revolutions, leaving streaks of foam behind. When meeting at the dividing line, they will have attained quite a respectable speed, bumping and hitting in the endeavor to push one another farthest from the line. The engagement often proves an exciting one. Of course the side is victorious which has the greater number of ships in the enemy's waters after the cruel war is over.

But no matter what the other entertainment may be, children anticipate and frankly enjoy the good things to eat. My experience was doubtless not unique at one party, when at the end of a rollicking game, and while preparing for another, I felt a soft hand slip into mine and heard the whisper: "But, auntie, when are we going to have *the party?*"

A "THREE-YEAR-OLD" PARTY

By K. C. H.

When Eleanor was three years old we decided to avoid the excitement of a birthday party and celebrate with a tiny dinner party. Two little girls, of three summers each, were the guests. Several days before the birthday baby was thrown into excitement over the lovely pink baskets mamma was making, and her first thought when she awoke on her birthday morning was to give mamma three sweet kisses and one to grow on, and to remark, "Now I don't have to wait any longer for my basket." The baskets were made of pasteboard, covered with pink crepe paper and lined with cream colored paper. Each basket was filled with choice candies. In the center of each was a tiny nest made of packing moss. Three candy eggs peeped from each little nest. These were the favors, and three childish hearts were made glad by them. Mamma made a lovely pink and white marble cake, icing it in white and covering it with pretty pink candies; three little candles sent their congratulatory beams to the little hostess from this pinnacle of sweets. A pedestal of flowers held the cake, and very beautiful it looked. Friends sent in bouquets, so the table was bright with flowers. The number three was made prominent, deviled eggs, butter, etc., all being served from small plates each holding three. The potato nests were very cute. Three small plates were set on the ice, butter was put in a coarse cheesecloth and pressed through in the shape of a ring. When dinner was served three small potatoes were put in each ring of . butter and speckled with coarse pepper. These delighted the children. How each little maiden trembled with importance as she touched the match to one of the candles, and how grown-up they felt, to sit in chairs at the table, without bibs, waited on like ladies; and ladies they were, behaving with decorum and still enjoying the new feature with true childish delight.

BOYS' AND GIRLS' PARTIES

BOYS' AND GIRLS' PARTIES

WALKING LETTERS

By Mary Dawson

A N excellent game for young people from six to eleven years is called Walking Letters. The idea made its debut a few weeks ago at a child's party in New York. The children present are formed into two bands or sides, each band containing exactly the same number of players. The bands are separated when the game is about to begin, each side taking up its position in one end of the room. Lots are drawn to decide which band will be first to choose a letter. The side drawing the slip marked "Begin" consult among themselves and choose a letter—any letter in the alphabet, from A to Z. The letter is kept strictly secret from members of the opposing band and is walked by one of the beginning side, who takes up his position in the center of the floor, and forms the letter by walking about in any direction necessary to describe an imaginary character upon the carpet. Each letter is walked three times, very slowly and carefully. If the opposing party can guess its name, a point is won for their side and chalked upon the blackboard where score is kept. If they fail to guess it, nothing is won, and the turn passes to the opponents, who now endeavor to guess a second letter outlined by one of those who were formerly guess-

ers. And so the fun goes on until each side has had
plenty of chances. When the guessing side wins a point,
that is, when they guess the letter correctly, they may
demand other letters, and go on guessing and winning
until they lose a point, when the turn reverts to the
opponents.

Numbers can be walked as well as letters, and will
be found to make a pleasant deviation in the long game.
Walking Letters offers a suggestion for an afternoon
party which can be arranged for in half an hour by using
the idea and securing a few pretty things for prizes.
Members of the side winning the most points draw
among themselves for the first prize. It is just as well
to have inexpensive consolation gifts on hand for all who
fail to win a trophy, thus preventing a lot of disappointment.

A BIG GAME HUNT

By Mrs. Paedagogue

When my yearly problem of getting acquainted with
the senior class faced me last fall, it seemed to me that
there was nothing new under the sun. But in October
we had our "big game hunt," a very nonsensical evening, and yet we had a good time and got acquainted.

My invitation had a little oval picture of President
Roosevelt in the upper left-hand corner and was written
and read like this: "To meet President Theodore Roosevelt's ideas and to follow his example, the pleasure of
Miss Brown's company is requested for a Big Game

Hunt, Friday evening, October 17, 1902, to start from 12 Main street promptly at 7.30 o'clock. Personally conducted by Mr. and Mrs. Paedagogue."

When our guests came, they assembled in our large living room, where there were seats for the greater part of them. This room had little in the way of decorations; just a few branches of hemlock in the electroliers, and boughs of oak and maple over the mantel and the portieres. A big fire was laid in the fireplace, ready to light. We chatted all together until about 8 o'clock, when I cast my eye over the company and saw the usual formation—nearly every one of the boys in a solid phalanx on one side of the room. Surely it was time to start the hunt.

The company was made up of thirty-two high school seniors, the six assistant teachers, Mr. Paedagogue and me. The teachers were the ministering angels who helped me all through the evening. At 8 o'clock they gave to each of our guests a little game bag which we had made for them. In each bag was a score card and pencil. Then I explained to the young people that all through the vicinity were many game animals, chiefly concealed in the woods. They were to have twenty minutes to hunt them, then they were to report their scores, according to the tally cards, and the largest scores should have prizes. We drew the curtains aside, throwing open the study, the dining room and the conservatory, which had a really woodsy appearance. Each room was lighted by only one bulb, and that covered with green tissue paper and surrounded with hemlock branches. In every corner stood a little tree of oak or hemlock; screens covered with maple boughs were arranged to make aisles and groves. In the twigs and branches and in any other good hiding places in the rooms, hidden as effectively as possible, were five pounds of animal crackers.

As soon as Mr. Paedagogue wound the hunting horn, the guests began the hunt with enthusiasm. The funny little animals were put into the game bags as captured, and in twenty minutes the hunting horn called the hunters from the forest. The tally cards were written like this: Lion twenty, tiger twenty, bear twenty, hippopotamus twenty, wild goat ten, wild sheep ten; all other animals, five each. Each hunter reported his own score, and then the prizes were awarded. The boy and the girl having the highest scores had each a little silver stickpin in the form of a fox's head; and the consolation prize was a bag of salt—to put on the tails of the animals, of course.

After ten minutes' chat, the teachers distributed to each of the boys and girls a sheet of manila paper, about sixteen by twenty-four, a colored crayon, a card having the names of forty animals and a little card having the names of one of these animals and a number. Every guest was asked to draw on his sheet of paper a picture of the animal named on his little card, and to attach its number. On the study table was a dictionary, open at pictures of animals, and when a boy told me that he couldn't remember how a camelopard looked, I referred him to the book. So in ten minutes the pictures began to come in, and I hung every one "on the line," or the wires which were stretched the length of the living room. After a little time to admire the works of art, the guests were asked to attach numbers to the names of animals on their score cards, thus guessing what each drawing represented. There was a good deal of fun in this.

After time had been given to put a number after each name on the score card, the lists of what they were intended to represent were read. Again the winners had simple little prizes: he, a china pointer dog; she, a photographic reproduction of a lion's head, mounted passe-partout. The booby was an animal alphabet-book. The names were written on the score card, as some of the drawings would be hard to identify.

Next came supper. We had taken forty little wooden plates, such as are sold for picnics, and on two of them drawn, with a few lines of sepia, lions' heads, on two others, elephants; and so on, until we had twenty pairs, which we divided into two sets of twenty plates each. We distributed one set of these to the boys, the other to the girls, and thus the boys found their mates for supper. When the partners were found and the company seated, a part of the boys on piazza cushions on the floor, my ministering angels passed the very simple picnic luncheon—sandwiches, stuffed eggs, coffee, crullers and cheese, and olives and pickles. I was not able to get for my coffee the tin cups that I wanted but I did get sturdy mugs, suitable for any camp; and the napkins were paper ones. After luncheon, the fire was lighted, and, as we sat watching the climbing flames, glowing yellow and green with driftwood, I had all the lights turned off, leaving the room with no illumination save the fire and Mr. Paedagogue's low reading lamp, with its dark shade. Beside the lamp sat Mr. Paedagogue, and as we watched the firelight, he read—and Mr. Paedagogue *can* read—the last few pages of The Trail of the Sandhill Stag.

Then two boys of the class came in, each with a cushion under one arm and a banjo under the other, seated themselves on the floor and struck up In the Good Old Summer Time, which has been a rally song of the class ever since the ditty came out. All the class took it up at once and sang it through. Until 10 o'clock they sang college and other popular songs. Then the players stopped and the lights were turned on.

This entertainment might have been burdensome had I not shared the work with the teachers. A week before the party I gave the forty plates to four of the teachers, and each made five pairs, taking the little sketches of animals' heads from the margins of Thompson-Seton's books. The other teachers wrote the score cards. Wednesday before the party we had a "bee" and made the game bags with the help of my sewing machine. Mr. Paedagogue and I had cut a part of them the evening before, so the basting and stitching began at once; we were all busy, there was no waiting and we finished them in three hours, besides drinking a pot of tea. The bags were made of khaki, or something much like it, the class color being yellow.

The little pencils are a considerable item of expense, and it would be just as well to pass common pencils when the score is called for. The afternoon of the party we arranged the rooms in something less than two hours. Mr. Paedagogue had two of the boys bring us a load of boughs, hemlock, oak and maple. The largest ones—little trees—we stood in the corners; the smallest we put in the electroliers. The rest we tied together in pairs by the ends, near the tips of the boughs, leaving about six inches of cord between them. I borrowed several screens and made aisles of them in each room, then hung the pairs of boughs by these cords over the tops of the screens, a branch on each side. Large boughs are always so satisfactory a decoration; the foliage is always graceful, and they are quickly put up and taken down.

EASTER FUN AND EASTER FEASTING

By E. M.

A party given last year for a crowd of boys and girls home on the Easter vacation was full of new ideas for entertaining at this season. All of them could be adapted for older people if desired. The invitations were lettered in green and violet on paper eggs, for which ingenious egg-shaped envelopes had been made by the hostess. Easter colors were even secured in the outside of the invitations by writing the address in violet ink and obeying Uncle Sam's behest by using two green one-cent stamps. The invitation read:

"Elizabeth Evans,
 Eight to Eleven,
 Easter Evening.
 Eggs, Euchre, Edibles."

The guests found reception rooms decorated in white, green and purple. The young hostess was aided in receiving by three delighted little sisters, each one in a ballet-like, white frock fringed about the edge of the skirt with purple violets and their leaves. The crowd of jolly young people were divided. Those who wished to play euchre each received a tiny basket, not unlike a nest, lined with fine straw. It was designed to hold the counters, which consisted of purple eggs for the winners, pale green ones for the losers. "Green with envy" was the epithet bestowed on a booby who retired from the game with not a single purple egg in the nest.

The young folks who decided in favor of games instead of cards, had all sorts of fun awaiting them. One frolic went on in the big attic, where a strange, maze-like path two feet wide had been whitened with chalk. It wound in and out behind trunks, among old furniture and barrels, sometimes perilously near the stair head, or into corners where had to follow it with stooping shoulders. This white path was an egg-rolling alley, and the rollers were the boys and girls who found themselves partners by the color of the eggs they had chosen. The eggs had been hard boiled, then dyed. There were two of each shade, and when the young folks drew them from the depths of a long bag, they took the color which luck ordered. A monitor stationed in the attic with a paper of rules started the game, each color coming in a certain order. The egg-rolling couple were armed each with a long-handled wooden spoon, such as a housewife uses to stir her pickles and preserves. The eggs were started very carefully and coaxed or tapped along, using the spoons as bats. The contest lay in keeping the eggs from rolling off the chalked path. As soon as one rolled over the edge, that spooner was out of the game until a turn came again, for in succession each one had three chances at the attic egg-rolling. It was great fun, even if only three came out winners, for the contest was anything but an easy one.

Another delightful half hour was spent over a hen and chicken game, something after the same idea which obtained at donkey parties years ago. At one end of a room well cleared of furniture, was tacked a big sheet of paper on which there was a clever, although rough, sketch in colored chalks of a clucking mother hen, a straw nest and a number of chipped eggs. To each boy and girl was given a roughly executed watercolor sketch of a little chicken cut out from heavy paper; to the back was attached a gummed wafer. It was also numbered, that number belonging till the game was over to the boy or girl who had drawn the chicken. In their turn, according to the number, a player was blindfolded, ordered to start at the tinkle of a bell in the direction of the hen and her eggs, and moistening the paper wafer, stick the chicken on, as near an egg or the mother hen as possible. Each player, still blindfolded, was led to a chair to sit in darkness till the game was finished. The result, when all were able to use their eyes, was uproarious shouts of laughter. Some of the little chickens sat on the top of the mother hen's head, one hung perilously head first from the point of her beak, some were climbing up her well feathered sides, while others lay in the straw kicking their heels in the air, or they blotched an eggshell out of existence. Two prizes were given to the players who had perched a chick in the most ridiculous place, the number on the back of the paper chick denoting the winner.

Another frolic, just before supper was announced, consisted of an egg hunt. This time the eggs were of the gourd variety. They were tucked away in every possible hiding place which could be found in a parlor and sitting room. Only one hunter at a time was allowed to go searching, the others were shut out in the hall. The hostess carried a memorandum of where the eggs had been hidden, and accompanying the searcher she clapped her hands slow or fast as the hunt waxed cold or hot. Each egg bore in gold letters the name of a guest, and if the wrong one was found it was returned to its hiding place, the hunt continuing till each one found an egg that bore its owner's name. It was found that the top of each gourd egg had been removed, then covered with a lid of paper and plaster of paris. Inside were tiny favors, a thimble, a daintily dressed wee doll, a strawberry emery, a pincushion, a button-hook, a stickpin, a ribbon, collar buttons, anything Lilli-putian enough to be hidden in an egg.

The appearance of the supper table was greeted with hearty cheers. It appealed to the artistic sense of a group of happy young folks as well as to their appetites. In the center of the table over a mat of asparagus ferns, a little wheelbarrow filled with candy eggs was drawn by two frolicsome brown rabbits, cutting up all sorts of didoes. The driver was a yellow chicken with a pair of reins in its beak. From this centerpiece radiated purple and green ribbons to each place, ending in a little mat of asparagus and a few stray violets. In the center of each sat a Humpty Dumpty egg, dressed with a tissue paper headdress to cartoon each young guest. The dudish boy's Humpty Dumpty wore an imitation silk hat, the girl who went in for golf found an egg wearing a droll little tam-o'-shanter. The boy who had won the title of "Stupid" in school discovered his place by an egg with a dunce cap, while the football lad's egg needed no hat, it was liberally thatched with a crop of un-combed excelsior.

The menu was simple enough, but excellent. There was a splendid array of sandwich plates, each one bearing at the side a brown candy rabbit with its ears pricked up and holding aloft on a paper banner a sandwich name, egg, chicken, lettuce, tongue, ham, nuts, or what-ever the filling might be. The ice cream was delight-fully served, and the conceit was a homemade one. From sheets of sponge cake had been cut oblongs, which did duty as small wagons, with tiny sponge cake rounds stuck in by toothpicks to look like wheels at the four corners. Each wagon bore a big white ice cream egg, molded with two spoons from the hard frozen mixture.

TWO JOLLY EVENINGS

By M. Louise Shaw

One rainy autumn day gave promise of such a disagreeable evening, I thought it would be pleasant to plan a little amusement for my brother, younger sister and a cousin who was visiting us. After a few moments' thought I gathered several magazines and cut from them the most interesting looking illustrated advertisements, carefully clipping from them all lettering which might afford a clue as to what they were to advertise. I intended to use about thirty, but found so many that I liked, some clever drawings, others ridiculous, and some excellent puzzles, that my final number was fifty. I then numbered each illustration with a good-sized figure and made a numbered list of the advertisements. This list of course was for my own use.

In the evening while we sat by the fireplace eating fudge, I produced my clippings and gave several to each, together with a slip of paper bearing fifty numbers, and a pencil, telling them to guess what the illustrations advertised and to write the name of each beside the corresponding number on the slip given them.

Interest was aroused at once and did not diminish throughout the evening. At last all were guessed but five or six, which were declared to be too puzzling. Then I read the correct list aloud. Some of the guesses were wrong, but not surprising. One picture of a smiling maiden eating bonbons was thought to advertise a particular brand of chocolates, while in reality it was her shining teeth disclosed to view which gave the key to the illustration. Those with the double meanings caused the most amusement. As no comparisons were made during the contest, the lists differed much.

Another evening we spent in a pleasant way. I wrote on four slips of paper the initials of us four, one set on each slip. Beneath these I wrote a list of ten questions, as follows, leaving a space below each one: 1. Description of this person? 2. What is his favorite amusement? 3. Chief characteristics? 4. Usual occupation? 5. Favorite books? 6. Chief virtue? 7. Greatest fault? 8. Greatest talent? 9. Chief dislikes? 10. Greatest ambition? After giving each a card bearing a set of initials *not* his own, I asked each to fill out in the space below an answer to each question containing three words, each word commencing with the initials on the card held, in their correct order. For illustration, take the initials of Charles Dana Gibson, and suppose we answer Question No. 4: "What is his usual occupation?" Answer: "Cleverly Drawing Girls." Much amusement was afforded later in the evening when we exchanged cards, and each read aloud what somebody else had written about another somebody else. Many were the sly but good-natured allusions to the little tricks and fancies known to be characteristic of the owner of the initials. In the corner of each card I had made a little sketch and each now serves as a souvenir of a pleasant evening.

PARTIES FOR GROWN-UPS

PARTIES FOR GROWN-UPS

THE DICKER PARTY

By Natalie Bell

A "DICKER PARTY" is an amusing function much in vogue the past summer at Bar Harbor and some other northern resorts. The guests bring from one to a dozen articles with which they are willing to part. These are carried about, well displayed by their respective owners, thus provoking conversation in plenty. "What have you that I want?" says A, meeting his best friend B, who is decorated with a bunch of striped and dotted, plaid and plain neckties of every hue. "That depends upon whether you have anything that I'll take," retorts B. And this is the sociable spirit of the dicker party. Each one examines the other's merchandise, and "dickers" if pleased. Sometimes a certain article will be dickered from one to another until it has been the successive property of every person in the room. Many laughable exchanges occur.

A popular artist was a guest at a gay little hotel where a dicker party was held and where everyone knew everyone else. So this gentleman brought to the fray at least half a dozen pairs of trousers, worn and weather-beaten, old hats and caps, and pipes galore; all of which he dickered away to the belles of the house in exchange for gay ribbons till he resembled a fluttering Maypole.

Stickpins, hatpins, handkerchiefs, laces, hats and wraps, collars, buttons and buckles, sashes, books, penholders, fans, vases and mugs, pincushions, bric-a-brac, anything and everything, even candy, appeared for exchange. One lady of quick and artistic impulse, who had just arrived at the hotel, took from her trunk a large flat hat she had intended to use for the sun and trimmed it gorgeously, in about ten minutes, with natural flowers and huge bows of pink and white tissue paper. It "took" immensely, and was soon dickered off for a cunning lace collar. The second owner appeared in it at breakfast the next day.

Given a good-sized party of friendly and fun-loving people, I cannot think of anything more really amusing than the dicker party. Why could it not be **given, by invitation,** in aid of small charities?

A HAP-HAZARD ROOF PARTY

By Camilla J. Knight

The invitations read, "A hap-hazard roof party," and the hostess agreed to "furnish the hazard." The guests were requested to wear old clothes, and two of the boys responded so literally that most of the girls refused to be seen near them for a moment. As the hostess lived in the upper flat of a small apartment house, the roof was the most comfortable place for entertaining in the summer. A large old carpet was spread on the gravel, with as many seats as possible placed around it.

Coming up the stairs, the guests followed sign-boards pointing "To the half-way house," as the flat was labeled, and there they met the hostess, who directed them to the "summit." On the roof door was the placard, "Consult dramatis personae first." But it was a long time before they found it, because, in hunting, they stopped to read so many other signs, such as "Keep off the grass," "Ten dollars' fine if you pick the flowers," "To the cave" (the fancy tower in front), "To the animals," "To the toboggan slide" (the stairway roof, also labeled "Out of repair").

Hammocks, chairs, parapets, chimneys, had appropriate remarks on them, the steamer chair, for instance, bearing "This chair for the oldest guest." There were forty-three different signs, made with a brush and ink on wrapping paper. A unique document of considerable length, tacked on one of the chimneys, told the story of the evening, and brought in the name of every guest, some in the style of "hidden names," others as puns, execrable or excusable. The title and beginning were as follows:

"Reid and Ponder

"At the Ring-ing of the Belle, we have come here from our Holmes, sweet Holmes, to-(K)night, to sit awhile side by Sidey, for a season of perfect Bliss, as we meet Mo's(ch)eldom than we could wish," etc., etc., the names being written heavily in red ink.

Finally reaching "dramatis personae," the guests found their duties clearly defined. All entered into the spirit of the thing, and made the affair a brilliant success. A former resident and a recent bride were guests of honor. The acrobats performed vaudeville gymnastic feats; the mounted police immediately climbed to the top of the chimney; the bureau of information, with his henchman at his heels, stalked about with an air of profound knowledge; and the mistress of the robes naively inquired, "Shall I put the robes in the bureau?" The keeper of the animals strolled about with a basket of animal crackers, when she was not guarding a corner where was a rare and curious collection of toy animals of various sizes, races and colors, many of them showing signs of a "previous condition of servitude."

The utmost tact had been used in assigning these parts, the hostess putting her own name down as one of the court fools. The trumpeters were supplied with tin whistles; the sky managers, with opera glasses, to look for the moon, which was scheduled to appear at 9 o'clock. As it was the last of June, and in a northern city, the daylight lasted till then. But the moon was the only one who went back on us. She appeared on time, but almost immediately hid her face behind some light clouds, and refused to show herself again.

The commissary-general and her assistants being ready to serve the refreshments, a lamp and a candle were brought up to aid in the proceedings. Plenty of lemonade in common glasses, and hundreds of sponge drops, were all the refreshment provided. Picnic plates, paper napkins and straws, besides being very cheap, added greatly to the fun, which momently became faster and more furious. The acrobats volunteered assistance as waiters, one of them leading the way with the candle placed on the end of an old broom.

Finally, a baby at home came suddenly to the recollection of one of the guests, and soon all were leaving. Someone said: "How are you ever going to get all these things down stairs?"

"Well, you might each 'take something before you go,'" suggested the hostess.

The hint was sufficient. When she entered her parlor, a few minutes later, her eyes were greeted by a pyramid of chairs and pillows, and a crowd of young people pressed around to assure her what a delightful time they had had at what someone termed "your burlesque lawn party!"

A MONOTYPE PARTY

By Lydia A. Smith

A very pleasant and novel way of entertaining a small company for an afternoon is to give a monotype party. Let the hostess provide for each participant a piece of common zinc about five by six inches; and a bristol brush, about a No. 3, also a medium-sized sable brush; one large tube of ivory black oil paint will be enough for the company, and two or three sheets of monotype paper. If the latter is not obtainable, as is often the case, the picture can be printed on the back of cheap wall paper; the less color, of course, the better. This seems to take the impression better than any other

A MEADOW IN MONOTYPE

paper, as there is no glaze, it is of the right weight, and is usually the mellow cream tint so desirable in the work, making a nice tone for the background. Some old, soft cloths are necessary for cleaning, and turpentine for thinning the paint.

We used the large dining room table for working, covering it first with heavy manila paper, that there might be no accidents. First select the subject for reproduction. This can be a photograph or print of any kind, the chief requisite being simplicity, as the main beauty is the balance of light and dark. The work must be in masses, and more suggestion than detail; in fact, there can be but very little detail in the picture.

To commence work, squeeze out some of the black paint, either on a palette or plate, then paint the entire surface of the zinc, very lightly, and with the fingers rub this smooth and fine, making a thin, uniform tint or tone all over. Take out the high lights with a bit of cotton on the end of a stick or brush handle. For instance, if the subject selected is a moonlight scene with clouds, trees and a glimpse of water, first take out the high lights in the clouds; if there are dark shadows, paint them in, using the fingers to form them into cloudlike shapes. Next the trees against the background or sky; these can be painted in masses suggestive of the growth, unless it is the case of an individual tree, like the pine, which is the principal object in the picture. Then it should be worked up with a little more detail. The foreground can be laid in with the brush and modeled with the fingers, taking out suggestive growth

A MOONLIT LAKE

near the edge of the picture (this can be done with the point of a stick), cutting out grasses, etc. Most of the modeling is done with the fingers. Take out the reflection of the moon on the water in the same manner as the clouds; and the moon must be taken out also, being very careful as to shape. To finish the edge, hold the plate or zinc with one hand and with the cloth over the thumb on the other hand, wipe out a tiny edge around the zinc, making rather a sharp line with the thumb nail. This gives a very nice finish, suggestive of a fine print or etching. Now our picture is ready to print and this must be done with a common clothes wringer.

Fasten the wringer to the back of an old chair, if there seems to be no other available place. This may be inconvenient, but the effort in holding the chair down, and the wringer steady, usually tends to break any ice that may have existed in the company. First a heavy blotter, say nine by twelve inches, is caught by the edge in the roller of the wringer. The other edge should be held by someone to keep it firm and even. Upon this is placed the zinc, paint side up. Now the paper on which the picture is to be printed should be saturated with water. If the monotype paper is used it can be laid flat in a shallow dish of water and left for a few minutes; if the wall paper be used, it is best to lay it flat (printed side down) and wash the back over either with a sponge or a bit of absorbent cotton. When ready for printing, put the blotter on it for an instant to remove the superfluous water, then lift by the corners and place on the painted zinc, being sure there are no wrinkles in the paper, which should be about eight by ten inches. Over the zinc and paper place the other blotter, holding it firm and steady. Run the whole

A FAVORITE SUBJECT

through the wringer, thus transferring the picture painted on the zinc to the paper. Only one impression can be successfully printed, as the zinc has to be repainted for each picture. When through the wringer place on the table, remove blotter and carefully peel off the printed paper. Place where it will dry and the picture is ready for mounting. This can be done now or later.

When ready to mount the picture place it face downward on a clean surface, dampen the back and put

MORE MOONLIGHT

paste around the edges (library paste is best). Then lift carefully and mount in the center of heavy cardboard. The picture will shrink quite a bit, hence the necessity for heavy cardboard; if a light weight is used, the picture will not look so well when mounted, as the shrinkage will draw the cardboard, unless it is heavy enough to stand the strain.   Use a thick mat of unglazed, creamy-toned paper and a very simple oak frame.

As a rule these little parties are very satisfactory, as each guest has a bit of his own work, and as there is no detail work to be carried out, the picture is easily made and is generally appreciated.   These are pretty Christmas gifts.   It is pleasant to have prizes awarded.

A GROWN-UP CHILDREN'S PARTY

By Augusta Kortrecht

Society has introduced as the newest way of having a good time, the child's party—not for the little folks, oh, dear, no, but for those grown-ups who wish to go back to pinafores and knickerbockers just for one night. The invitations must plainly request that the guests be dressed as children, so that there will be uniformity, for nothing dampens the ardor of a costume party like a sprinkling of persons not in character.   A very fitting sentiment for the invitations is:

"Backward, turn backward, O Time, in your flight,
   Make me a child again just for to-night."

If you receive an invitation to such a party, and for any reason cannot enter into the spirit of the thing and put off your long skirts and dress suit, then politely decline by all means, and save both yourself and the others the unpleasantness of having a misfit in the circle.

If you do go, then make yourself a child as nearly as possible.   The women must be little girls, hair down, either curled or tied back in some youthful fashion, and dresses short; and the men must be small boys, in short trousers or juvenile looking sailor suits.

The games for this party are the old ones you used to play, "stage coach," "button, button, who's got the button?" etc. Recitations are suitable, and dancing, both fancy figures and the round and square dances. Anything that can accent the juvenile effect adds to the fun. If paper and pencil games are liked, the following is new and amusing: Each person draws a picture of some scene from Mother Goose, then passes the paper on to the right-hand neighbor, who looks at the drawing and writes below what he guesses it to represent. The guess is covered by folding a tuck in the slip of paper, leaving the drawing visible, and the next person makes his guess, keeping this up until everybody has guessed on each picture. A prize may be given for the artist whose picture received the most correct guesses, and also a booby prize makes the fun livelier.

The supper table, of course, must have more elaborate dishes than one for a party of real children, but the decorations should carry out the idea of the illusion. Any pretty centerpiece will do—a gorgeous doll in a bower of blossoms, a toy automobile filled with fruits, or just a flower piece, which is always in good taste. If rather handsome favors are to be given, silver spoons and little silver pushers are suitable; but more frequently tiny dolls for the little girl-ladies and chocolate cigars for the small boy-gentlemen are used. There should be small bibs at each place instead of napkins, and if possible the china should be the gaily decorated patterns which are brought on for children.

The popping mottoes which are seen at all uppers for the youngsters are very nice here, and the caps will be worn with almost as much joy as if it were all a novelty to the merrymakers.

A CINDERELLA PARTY

By Mabel Philpott

A Cinderella dancing party may be made very enjoyable. The invitations might have a dainty French slipper painted in water-color in one corner, or simply the word "Cinderella." After the guests assemble and before the dancing commences, let them understand thoroughly the hour to cease: 10, 11 or 12. If not too late for them, 12 would be appropriate. Have a clock with a loud, clear gong which all can hear, and the moment it strikes, all dancers must take part in the slipper hunt. For this buy a pair of doll slippers, and hide one slipper in one room, while the mate is hidden in another. Guests should separate, ladies taking one room, gentlemen another. The youth who finds the slipper should go to the other room and find the maiden who holds its mate, and to these lucky ones should be given prizes. This couple of course will be partners at the supper which follows. Among the rest distribute slippers cut from fancy stiff papers, only two of each kind being made. On one put this:

Ye prince, who hold this slipper in hand,
Go make a search through this merry band,
And find ye a maiden whose tiny shoe
Is a mate to the one now held by you,
     And claim your Cinderella.

On its mate put this verse:

Ye Cinderella, who hold this shoe,
Someone now is looking for you,
So keep your slipper and patiently wait
Till comes the prince who has found its mate,
     And claims his Cinderella.

Distribute these among the dancers, then serve
refreshments. As far as I know this is original and
will have at least the merit of being "something new."

FOR CARD PARTIES

A very pretty color scheme was carried out in
serving the refreshments at a card party. After the
game was finished, the guests retained their seats, dainty
lace and embroidered cloths were spread, and a candlestick bearing red, green or yellow candles, according to
the color of the room, was placed on each table. In the
green room delicious fruit salad was served in hollowed
out green apples; a sandwich of brown bread, cut cres-
cent shape, and a round sandwich of white bread with
two olives were on the plate. In the red room the salad
was served from red apple shells. In the yellow room

oranges hollowed out held the salad, salted nuts were passed, tutti frutti ice cream was served in tall glasses. The plates for the red room had a red tulip, the yellow tulips found their way to their proper room, while those in the green room found a spray of giant mignonette on their plates. This was a most clever conceit and really very little trouble.—E. H. G.

At a recent card party the hostess puzzled her guests by providing beans as tallies, instead of paper stars and hearts. Five beans were awarded to the winners, at the end of each game, and one to the losers, each one being solemnly warned to keep his beans carefully in a little bag provided for the purpose. There was much conjecture during the games as to the ultimate use of the beans, but no hint was given until, as the tallies for the last game were being distributed, a maid brought in dainty bills of fare bearing the following astonishing information:

Sandwiches,	5 beans
Coffee,	3 beans
Almonds,	5 beans
Olives,	5 beans
Ices,	10 beans
Cakes,	5 beans

Immediately there was anxious diving into bags to count up accumulated gains, and more anxious calculations by those who were short of funds as to what their store would buy. Some of the fortunate, who had seven beans more than the cost of the entire bill of fare, generously offered to share with their poorer neighbors, but when it was found that even that would not treat everyone to the entire menu, the hosts offered to advance, for forfeit, enough to make up each deficiency. This was accepted, and later on the forfeits were redeemed, which was amusement enough for the rest of the evening.—Mrs. W. H. MacColl.

A PUMPKIN PARTY

By Mrs. W. A. Harvey

We decorated square white cards with a huge pumpkin. The hostess who cannot draw can cut a very presentable pumpkin from orange paper and paste it on the cards. We wrote on each card: "The mammoth pumpkin will be on exhibition at Mrs. B.'s from 1 to 11 p. m. next Thursday. You are cordially invited to come and guess its weight." We got the largest pumpkin we could find and a collection of medium-sized ones. We made a record of the weight, the length and the girth of the big pumpkin. We carefully cut it open lengthwise, scooped it out and counted the seeds. We then filled it with sawdust and buried in it inexpensive souvenirs—orange-hued penwipers, needlebooks, pincushions, etc., wrapped in paper. We set the pumpkin on a mat of leaves on a small table and labeled "hands off." Each guest was given a card

with a pencil attached, to record his guesses. **Pumpkin-**
shaped paper weights, inkstands, emery bags and blot-
ters pleased the prize-winners. The rest of the evening
was spent in carving jack-o'-lanterns from pumpkins.
The guest may be required to write a recipe for pumpkin pie, which will bring forth some wonderful flights
of fancy. The supper was served from pumpkin dishes.
Select round, deep pumpkins with a stem, choosing
those of a pretty color, any shape; saw off the tops
even so they may be put back on the pumpkins as
lids, scoop out and line with parchment paper.

TALLY CARDS

By A. J. L.

Some of the prettiest of tally cards are the red silk
pincushions made in the shape of hearts. Large white-
headed pins are used for the counts. Then, something
on the same idea, and nice for souvenirs afterward, are
tiny scent bags. These came to my notice at a card
party given by Princeton students. The bags were
very effective in their orange and black satin, and they
were fastened to black paper tallies by bunches of
orange ribbon. Japanese fans with strings hanging
from them are pretty. Big glass beads are strung on
the strings for counts. For the woman who doesn't
like to sew, but is quick with brush and pen, there
are almost unlimited possibilities. Among these pieces
of water color paper cut and colored to represent slices
of watermelon are odd and effective. There are holes

punched in the paper through which ribbons bearing
tiny black penny dolls, or pasteboard seeds, can be
fastened, according to the maker's taste. Then there
are cards upon which clippings from magazines may
be pasted. It is surprising what aid the advertising
section lends for this purpose. A few lines added in
ink make the little picture look almost like a pen and
ink sketch. The birch bark tally is a pretty reminder
of summer days. If the bark prove unruly, moisten
and press with a hot iron. Then cut it into hearts
and clubs, and use an ordinary card punch on the
tally the night of the card party.

A HAYSEED CARNIVAL

By D. A. W.

A new form of the fashionable barn party which
has been so popular during the past year or two is called
the hayseed carnival. It is the most informal function
imaginable, as the invitations first of all go to show.
These are written upon ruled paper and worded in the
quaint phraseology and bad spelling which suggests
Samantha Allen and Betsey Bobbett. Here is a short
example:

"Marietta Summer, she that was a Smith, wants all
her friends and nabers to come to the old red barn next
Thursday night for a reglar jollification. Every naber
as isn't sick-a-bed will be looked for.

"P. S. Please don't hev on your Sunday fixins."

The sports, which old people as well as young will
find it hard to resist, consist of a series of contests in

true country style. For the men there is a wood sawing contest, while the ladies pare potatoes or apples for a prize. Another sport in which both men and women join is match games of tit-tat-to on a blackboard. Husking corn, an old-fashioned spelling bee and a rousing Virginia reel are other features which make the rafters echo with fun. The refreshments are, of course, suited to the occasion. Wedges of apple pie, milk, doughnuts, cider, gingerbread and the like refresh the contestants when their labors are at an end.

TABLEAUS

By D. A. W.

A party of girls summering on Long Island had great success with a vaudeville entertainment. The hit of the evening was a dream picture called "the reveries of a bachelor." The scene represented a bachelor's den. A man with pipe and book sat musing in an arm chair before the fire. After a moment or two music began to play very softly and one by one the Reveries, always taking the form of pretty girls, drifted into the room. Each ghost disappeared after a moment or two to make room for another. The music was sometimes appropriate to the picture. Annie Laurie was played as a lovely Scotch girl appeared before his chair. The Girl I Left Behind Me brought a charming maiden in the quaint dress of "before the war" times. Other visions were The summer girl of 1902, The New York girl, The Gibson girl, The Stanlaws girl, Gibson's "widow" and The Quaker maid of Philadelphia.

AN OLD-FASHIONED CASTER UTILIZED AS A FRUIT DISH

A CHRYSANTHEMUM COTILLION

By Mary Dawson

Rooms and corridors were decorated with banks of chrysanthemums. Each of the young women invited came wearing a different shade of gown. Chrysanthemum shades only were worn, such as pink and white, dark and light yellow, and tints which deepened into or paled away into other tints as in the blossoms. Among the favors were shepherdess crooks, having bunches of chrysanthemums tied to the handles with streamers of ribbon; stickpins in the form of the flower of the evening; bonbonnieres decorated with chrysanthemum designs and long-handled wicker baskets filled with the blooms. A lovely figure devised by the hostess was called the chrysanthemum arch. This was formed by men and girls arranged in two lines facing each other and holding long-stemmed chrysanthemums. Other couples then waltzed through the bower thus formed. A variation of the popular "egg figure" was formed by substituting chrysanthemum flowers for eggs upon the floor, the object being to dance between these flowers without disturbing any. Ice cream was served in the form of yellow, white and pink "mums." Cake was passed in lovely little boxes, each having a design of the flower on the cover.

A WIGWAM DANCE

By Mary Dawson

The wooden platform erected for the dancing is draped and decorated to suggest the tepee. Blankets, bows and arrows, strings of beads, skin rugs, etc., are called into play; care being taken not to cut off the air from the platform by the arrangement of these. A pretty background for the platform is formed of green boughs and vines. Then, scattered here and there about the grounds, are tiny wigwams, made from rawhides arranged over poles. The hides are painted in rude hieroglyphics or pictures and fringed at the edges. Each little wigwam contains some refreshment for the dance. For one dance the favors are bows and arrows, and a charming little figure follows in which all dance, holding these trophies. Long eagle feathers, made respectively from gold and silver enamel, are the gifts in another round. They are donned by the dancers and worn during the rest of the evening. Among the other things distributed are chamois or buckskin cushions painted or "pyrographed" in appropriate designs; little bright articles beaded in the Indian-style; peace pipes, snow-shoes, moccasins, wampum belts, paddles, fancy baskets and miniature toboggans. The program for the evening ends with a "great medicine dance." In this the men join hands and circle round the girls, the girls afterward reversing things and dancing round the men. It is possible to serve ice cream from baskets of sweet grass and to have a table centerpiece for the supper in the form of a birch bark canoe filled with water lilies. Hatchet bonbonnieres filled with sweets are appropriate.

FEBRUARY PARTIES

By Mary Dawson

All the young unmarried folk are sure to welcome the idea of a partner's party, one of the latest in home entertaining. It affords an opportunity for any young man who feels attracted to a girl in the party to show his devotion by assisting her to win the ladies' game. At the same time the girl who desires to help any young man onward to the gentlemen's trophy may bend all her energies in that direction.

The game is progressive. Six or more tables—the number of these varying according to the number of guests—are arranged as for any ordinary card function. Any game from jackstraws to whist can be played at the tables. A different one at each table is best. Provide tallies for all the company. Lots are drawn before the opening of the game to decide where each competitor shall sit. One table should be arranged for four persons. Games are begun and finished by the ringing of a bell. Each person plays for himself, as single handed games are "required by the constitution." At the end of each game the girl and man who have won the most points are declared partners. These two write their names on each other's cards and progress to the next table. No stars are used on the tallies, and the sole idea of the progression is to become partners as many times as possible with the same person.

The man and woman who at the end of the rounds have written their names oftenest on each other's cards are declared victorious. The young man carries off the gentlemen's prize, while the ladies' honors are bestowed upon the lucky girl. Much fun is added by choosing prizes of a sentimental character. The game is followed by a supper to which the guests walk in a procession, led by the prize-winning partners. Each lady is placed at table beside the gentleman with whom she was oftenest joined in partnership.

A CIVIC EVENING

A bright New York girl gave a pleasant little entertainment not long ago which she christened a "civic party." Being a clever user of the kodak, she had in hand fifty views of New York city, all original work. The collection included public squares, civic buildings, libraries, banks, well-known corners of streets down town, the various park entrances, the Battery and Castle Garden, churches, philanthropic institutions. Each of the views was mounted upon a gray card and numbered. Pencils and paper were distributed and guests were asked to write down the name of each view as they supposed it to be.

Although all of the players were residents of New York or visitors from neighboring cities thoroughly familiar with it, the person winning the highest score did not name correctly more than half the views. Nor was this the fault of the photographs themselves, which were exceptionally clear and true. It was simply evidence of the well-known fact that the average citizen is capable of living years in a town without observing it carefully.

Try it, substituting your own town or the city nearest you. If you are not a photographer get twenty-five or fifty views from your book dealer or from magazines and newspapers. The names can easily be cut away and the photos mounted, numbered, etc.

WEDDING PARTIES

WEDDING PARTIES

A BRIDESMAIDS' TEA

By Marjorie March

FASHION dictates that the bride shall give a gift to her bridesmaids. The groom gives a farewell dinner to his ushers the night before the wedding; why not forestall their good time by giving a bridesmaids' tea in the afternoon? It can be made still more charming, an introduction to the wedding day, as it were, by the sending out of a few dainty notes by the bride herself to the one that is sure to obey her demands and to his friends, asking them to drop in for a cup of tea at 5 o'clock. Then for a few moments toward the end of the afternoon the bridesmaids and ushers can both pay homage to the queen of the morrow and to one another.

If the house is to be decorated the next day for the reception, it would of course be folly to have elaborate preparations; but great bowls of roses are simple in effect and require little arrangement. The present room can be arranged to be open so that the bridesmaids and ushers may be the first to view the gifts. As the whole affair should be informal to be enjoyable, the bride should be dressed in simple white, a rose in her hair and a few roses at her belt. Her mother should help her receive the few guests, and when all have arrived the tea should be served. Tea, iced and hot, chocolate, salad sandwiches, ices and cakes are what the occasion demands. If the grounds about the house are accessible it is a pretty idea to have the tea spread on a table on the lawn. The most interesting feature of the afternoon to the bridesmaids will be the receiving of their gifts. A pin is a very usual gift, and these can be pinned to the ribbon bows that tie a bunch of swaying roses that are placed at each bridesmaid's place. These bows of ribbon should be blue, for the bride must wear the traditional "something old, something new, something borrowed and something blue," and the setting of the tea table can carry out the same symbolical idea very easily. A good deal of fun can be occasioned by the guessing which article on the tea table is the borrowed one. The whole afternoon will be in a way a quiet, pleasant way of saying good-bye to the maid who to-morrow will become a new self, so there is little to suggest in the way of entertainment. When a dozen people get together who are friends and have real feeling in their hearts, there will be no lack of spontaneous merriment, and if even that joy has its note of sadness, so much the better.

A HAUSFRAU LUNCHEON

By Mary Dawson

One of the June brides who has returned from her wedding tour and gone to housekeeping had a novel luncheon given her the other day. It was called a *hausfrau* luncheon. Table setting, favors, et cetera, were all suggestive of the future good housekeeping. Instead of having a formal floral centerpiece, the table was decorated with little wooden tubs from the toy shop filled with water and having water lilies floating in them. The place cards, when examined, proved to be little autograph cook books with the names of guests written upon the covers. The bonbonnieres were market baskets filled with candies, and instead of a corsage bouquet each cover had a tiny feather duster tied with a knot of ribbon. Each little detail was suggestive in some way of the central idea. The result was a piquante little table.

A GOLDEN WEDDING

By K. C. H.

My parents' golden wedding anniversary occurring in August, I decided to celebrate by entertaining in their honor. "Our folks" are the kind of self-sacrificing old people who think that whatever is done for them is "too much trouble," so the affair was kept a secret from them. Our home was larger and better arranged, besides, I could entertain much more easily in my own home. I was doing my own work, my baby daughter was in her troublesome "second summer," and my trusted "better half" unavoidably absent; still, in spite of all these drawbacks, without a cent's expense (except for material) I entertained forty guests very pleasantly, and gave my dear old folks a dainty and agreeable surprise, that will give them pleasant memories until "memory is no more."

The invitations were written in gold ink, and read thus:

Mrs. Blank—

At home, three to five p. m.

In honor of Mr. and Mrs. Samuel Chapin.

Aug. 17, 1851—Aug. 17, 1901.

I don't know whether this was according to form or not, but the invitations looked very pretty. They were simply my calling cards, and saved considerable time. The house was put in order, the baking done, and such decorations as I could muster were put in place. By chance I had a bolt of rich yellow crepe paper, which I draped on mantels, etc. Yellow asters and nasturtiums were the flowers used, and most beautiful they looked, drooping over slender vases, or brightening a bank of green. Having only what my garden afforded, the supply was, of course, limited.

One of the decorative schemes I invented, and it proved a taking feature. In a secluded corner of the dining room I placed a small square table. On this I placed a large white, porcelain lined kettle. Around this I piled a few stones, green with moss, while a great quantity of asparagus was used to bank up around the kettle. A potted fern appeared to be growing just beside this mock spring. A friend gave me an old-fashioned gourd; this floated on the "spring," which was filled with fine lemon-orange punch, ice cold, and most refreshing. All the guests, except some relatives of the family, were old people, most of whom had knelt by cool New England springs in their youth, and this reminder of bygone days was quite effective. One old lady cried, saying that reminded her more of her "old New England home than anything else she had seen in Kansas." When the guests, old neighbors and fellow-pioneers of my parents, arrived, a carriage was sent to bring the aged bride and groom to my house "for dinner," as per arrangement.

Such a jolly company! A wonderful sadness came over me, seeing the aged and infirm putting aside the tales and memories of their strife and sorrows in this new land and recalling early pleasant memories and experiences. I had to put this feeling aside, however, and be a "smiling hostess." I have attended many gatherings, but never one of such genuine good feeling and real enjoyment. Each one seemed to feel that it was a gala day, and that nothing on his part must mar the beauty of it.

Refreshments were served on the lawn, consisting of ice cream and cake in considerable variety, the rich gold cake being most prominent. Here the speeches of congratulation were made and the gifts presented.

THE CELEBRATION OF WEDDING ANNIVERSARIES

By Marjory Pelton

One notices more and more in this country the fashion grow for celebrating the anniversary of a wedding. The observance of a diamond wedding, when two people have traveled life's road together for seventy-five years, has occurred at rare intervals, and has been the subject of national interest. Sometimes the diamond wedding is celebrated after sixty years of married life. That is incorrect, still it does happen, as if the aged couple had small hope of seeing the real diamond wedding. The golden wedding, a celebration of fifty years' happiness, is so frequent an occurrence that it speaks well for American longevity and the domestic peace of our nation. The earlier celebrations—the silver wedding to commemorate twenty-five years of married life, the china wedding for twenty years, the crystal wedding for fifteen years, the tin wedding for ten years, and the wooden wedding for five years—are daily occurrences everywhere.

There is another, the paper wedding, the first anniversary of a wedding day, which is occasionally observed among a group of young folks, who turn it into a merry-making. They come adorned with grotesque paper caps extracted from motto crackers and sometimes in entire costumes evolved from gorgeous crepe paper. The paper wedding offers an excellent chance for a masquerade party, when paper of all sorts may be utilized, from pert, pretty Yum-Yum with a Japanese parasol to a frolicsome youth representing the yellow kid in an impromptu suit made from yellow journals. There is the greatest latitude when it comes to gifts. The offering may be a dainty box of stationery or a book in the most artistic of bindings. For table decorations paper can be used lavishly, with paper table napkins, and even one of those beautiful tablecloths in paper which can be found in Japanese stores. Globes for gas and electricity, or lamps, can revel for that one night in wonderful paper shades, and where an artistic taste would demand flowers and wreathings of smilax or the delicate asparagus vines, it yields to the harmony of things and substitutes paper blossoms as true to nature as they can be found, with Japanese lanterns and lengths of paper ribbon for draping. If the decorator has fine taste, a house can be made really charming with paper decorations, if they are kept in delicate colors which harmonize. At the paper wedding, as in all other celebrations, the bride ought to wear her wedding gown, and after the passing of only twelve months, it is possible for her to be surrounded by her bridesmaids in their year-old frocks.

The young couple who, after five years' life together, can celebrate the wooden wedding in the summer and in the country can turn it into a delightful rustic affair. It may take the form of a picnic or evening lawn party. Birch bark can be utilized for writing invitations, for guest cards, menus and for the cover of a book in which the guests may write their names. Do not ruin the effect of an outdoor affair by spreading a tablecloth and using china or glass. The charm to a boarding school girl of a pound party is eating off a bare table and wooden plates. At a bakeshop purchase a liberal supply of thin wooden plates, and a rummage among friends ought to provide plenty of old-fashioned steel knives and forks with wooden handles. Serve everything on wood in chopping bowls, wooden trenchers, or in the thin, deep wooden trays in which a grocer sends lard or butter home. Let carving be done with wooden-handled knives, and serving be done with wooden spoons or forks, such as are seen accompanying a salad. Cups and saucers or tumblers and silver teaspoons are the only things which may have to be substituted for anything less rustic. Simply keep everything wooden as far as it is possible, except in guests. One "wooden" guest would spoil the jollity of a greenwoods feast. Wooden wedding gifts are indescribable in variety. There are writing desks, lead pencils, rocking chairs, potato mashers, or a clotheshorse.

Occasionally, when the mistress of a home has a spacious, spotless, well-appointed kitchen, she sets the table for the tin wedding supper there and gives the affair an old-fashioned spirit, such as one sees at a real country Thanksgiving. If you celebrate in this style, serve old-style dishes—beans and brown bread, doughnuts, pie of every sort, cider, raised cake, pickles, buckwheat cakes with maple syrup, lifted straight from the stove to the table, baked apples and coffee. Set style wholly aside for once. Serve the food on bright tin pie plates, the coffee in a tin pot, pouring it in tin mugs. Tin spoons and tin forks are the proper thing. Light the table with candles, set in tin candlesticks, and let the centerpiece be old-fashioned flowers set in a large tin pan. A dance to the rollicking old tunes that can be evoked by a country fiddler from his treasured violin, may round out a merry evening, with old country games interspersed between the Virginia reel and Thread the Needle. When it comes to the question of gifts for a tin wedding, my advice is to spend fifteen minutes in some big ten-cent store.

The crystal wedding suggests that the married couple are growing mature and leaving frolic and kissing games and dancing to a household of young folks. The crystal wedding is a parlor and dining room affair, where conventionality rules the day. The wedding gown may be donned again if it fits, but alas! as May Irwin sings in that heart-breaking ditty of hers:

> "The delicate waist of a day that is dead
> Will never come back to me."

There will probably be throngs of guests, handshaking, a flower adorned tea table, music, chatter and an array of cut glass that will gladden the heart of a housewife.

The china wedding may be conventional or not, as one desires to make it. The most delightful affair of this sort I ever attended was given by the mistress of an old-fashioned house, where we gathered for the afternoon with our sewing. There was gossip such as women love while the needle flies. Then there was an old-fashioned tea with delicious old-fashioned food, and we ate from rare china that one hundred and twenty years ago was a wedding present to our hostess's great-grandmother. It was a restful, pleasant, memorable party. Later, when the lamps were lit, our husbands arrived and cards were played, old songs were sung and old days recalled. Before leave-taking, we drank cider and ate loaf cake made from a recipe of fifty years ago.

The silver wedding means often a large family gathering, with one or two sweet grandchildren added to the circle, a silvering touch in the hair, hopes for the future and a look back on the joys and sorrows of twenty-five years. There is a table of gifts, which brings back the memory of the first wedding day, and the genial heartfelt wishes of long-tried friends. About the golden wedding there is a certain pathos. Amid all the festivity, in the gathering of children, grand-children, perhaps even great-grandchildren, and the offering of gifts, which cannot be bought for a trifle as in the merry-making days of youth—the hearts of the old bride and groom go back to the wedding day of fifty years ago, to the beloved ones who stood beside them; to the old home, to youthful hopes and—all that has come between. Then the eyes grow dim with tears. The golden wedding is the last milestone passed in the path which has been trodden so long together.

HALLOWEEN PARTIES

HALLOWEEN PARTIES

HALLOWEEN FROLICS

By Mary Dawson

A HALLOWEEN entertainment on new and lively lines is a future party. The games, as sports for the fateful eve should, unveil the future. The mysterious character of the festival is carefully preserved, but the divination is carried out in novel and unexpected ways. For example, one good feature is known as the book of fate. This is an enormous volume made of two dozen sheets of wrapping paper folded in half. The cover is of pasteboard decorated with India ink witches or goblins holding will-o'-the-wisp lanterns. The title, "Book of Fate," appears on the cover in black lettering. Each sheet has written upon it one letter of the alphabet, not arranged in rotation, but written at haphazard. Any letter may occur two or three times, if desired. The book, if consulted on Halloween, will reveal the initials of the person one is to marry. To consult it the fate reader must be blindfolded and a wand or divining rod be placed in his hand. With the rod he turns over the pages of the book. He turns twice only. The letters upon the pages turned are the characters he seeks. From them the name of the future companion must be guessed.

Then there is the Halloween pie, which is great fun, and not generally known. This can be played in two ways. For the first take a tub or basin and fill it with sawdust. Bury in the sawdust a number of slips of paper, each slip having written upon it a line of doggerel verse somewhat on the following order:

"Curly hair. Eyes blue. Roman nose. Tall and true."

"Small. Blond. Merry eyes. Inclined to plumpness. Witty. Wise."

"Tall. Dark. Somewhat sedate. Lovely lashes. True life mate."

There should be just as many slips in the pie as there are guests in the drawing room, and all rhymes should be equally applicable to either sex. The pan is covered with a shelving pasteboard crust tinted to make it resemble nicely browned pastry. Each guest in turn dips out for himself a huge spoonful of the pie. The description found in it is that of the future mate.

Another good game results if the pie is differently filled. For this tuck away in it a number of objects of many kinds and have some bright man or girl to act as fate interpreter. Each player spoons up a trifle for himself out of the pie, and the interpreter immediately explains its significance. The fun lies in the absurd interpretations, which are of course made to fit the case, and the little good-humored sallies to which the fate seeker exposes himself.

A NUTTING PARTY

The half dozen games on which a nutting party is founded can be arranged with a very trifling expenditure of time and labor. The opening game goes to decide the question of whether or not each player is destined to marry. This is played by making a little heap of nuts in some portion of the parlor and giving your guests each a broad-bladed kitchen knife. To discover his fate he must pick up one of the nuts upon the knife and run around the room with it so balanced. Two minutes is allowed for this feat. If he fails to get the nut on the blade, or if it tumbles in the progress round the room, the one thus failing will never marry.

To provide for each member of the party a description of the man or woman to come most prominently into his or her life, hide here and there around the room a number of nuts of different sorts. The hiding should be done before the company arrives. Each man or girl is told to look about the room for a nut. But instead of trying to discover and collect as many of these nuts as possible, as in a peanut search, each person stops looking after discovering his or her first nut. This nut will give the character of the husband or wife-to-be. The hostess acts as interpreter, reading the signs of the shell, the size and so on. Thus the girl who finds a black walnut will marry a man of good nature, but uncultivated and decidedly rough in exterior. He will be large, dark, unconventional and totally unsuited to the drawing room. The man who finds a hazel nut may be on the lookout for a tiny woman, round of figure, with brown hair and eyes. She will be smooth, gentle, without great strength of mind, but agreeable, cultivated and so on.

Another pretty feature for a nutting party is the nut tree. A small bush is used for the tree. From its branches hang a number of gilded walnut shells. Each shell has been split with a sharp knife, the meats removed and a humorous fortune placed inside, after which the shells are glued together. Players are blindfolded in turn and given a pair of scissors. Each man or girl clips a nut from the tree. The shell when broken reveals the future, which may be expressed in verse.

FISHING FOR FATE

A good way to play this game is over a high screen. On one side of the screen, hidden from view, sits the hostess, with a huge basketful of odds and ends which may be humorously interpreted into fates. On the other side of the screen stand the players, each armed with a fishing pole constructed simply of a cane and a yard of two of ribbon. The players take turns in casting lines over the screen, and each as he casts is obliged to say what he desires to draw up. Thus he may say: "I wish to know my state in life, whether married or single." Or "I wish to ascertain the personality of my future mate." The voice and the wish expressed both act as prompters to the hostess. By them she is able to tell whether the line belongs to a man or a woman and to make some absurd reply to the question. She deftly attaches an appropriate object to the ribbon and gives a little twitch which stands for a bite.

As a sample of the fateful articles to be pulled up, we will say that the young man who wishes to ascertain the personality of his bride-to-be may draw up a wax doll. This shows conclusively that he will fall victim to a girl of pretty face but not distinguished by mental capacity. If a man draws up a needlebook or a spray of bachelor's buttons he will of course remain a bachelor. The girl who pulls up a thimble is destined to old maidhood. She who draws up a bag filled with paper money will marry a rich man or receive a legacy. An empty pocketbook with a rose in it shows for the recipient a future of happiness and poverty.

To find out the length of time which will elapse before each member of the party is engaged, twelve candles, one for each month in the year, are lighted and arranged upon a table or the edge of the piano. Each young person is blindfolded in turn and told to blow out the candles. Three minutes is allotted for performing this feat. The number of candles remaining lighted when the three minutes have elapsed represents the number of months which are to intervene before the engagement takes place. If any man or girl fails to blow out a candle he or she will surely be bachelor or old maid. The girls who are thus destined to single blessedness can receive a match safe or other ornament in the form of a tabby, accompanied by Pope's apt and familiar couplet:

"How happy is the lonely vestal's lot.
The world forgetting, by the world forgot."

The doomed bachelor is given a "Hussif," to aid, it is explained, in sewing on his buttons.

A HALLOWEEN PARTY

By Augusta Kortrecht

The invitation I received was a tiny card with quaint lettering: "Come on Witch Night to ye House at ye Sign of Ye Black Cat"; and in one corner the hour and date, and the address of my hostess.

Five or six of us went in a body, and after we turned into Lindsay street, there was no missing the house we sought, for the sign of the black cat was to be seen afar off. It had been made of a big square pasteboard bonnet box; queer cat shapes were drawn in pencil on each of the four sides, then cut out with a sharp knife, and the openings pasted over with tissue paper from the inside. With a strong candle burning inside, the cats showed vaguely in the clever homemade lantern. The hostess told me afterward that she had experimented with black paper but had not found it thin enough to show the light through, and that therefore these cats were green and yellow. Each gate post bore one of these lanterns, while the front porch was hung with jack-o'-lanterns, made from pumpkins, of course.

The large transom of the front door had a curiously contorted cat cut from black paper or calico, and pasted on. The hall was well lighted to show this up to the guests approaching along the walk; but the rooms themselves were all in half dark, being illuminated only by lanterns like those on the gate posts.

We were greeted by two weird figures draped in white, and were shown to the dressing rooms and invited to deck ourselves in sheets and pillowcases. The hostess, the white figure which went with the ladies, showed us how to wrap the sheets around us and fasten them firmly with pins and pieces of tape, so that we were covered and yet had our arms somewhat free. White masks hid our faces, and pillowcases were fastened on top of our heads and left hanging down at the back. The white curtains of the dressing room were hung with bats, cut from black calico, and we were told to pin one of these on each of our sheets to distinguish us from the men, whom we found draped as ourselves, but wearing black snakes wriggling down their fronts.

It was very weird when we gathered again in the dim drawing room. The candles in the lanterns gave just sufficient light to show the ghost-like forms and the white hangings which were everywhere decorated with black calico snakes, lizards, bats, frogs, owls and cats. There were queer stuffed birds about in the corners; and live black cats of various sizes glided in and out, rubbing themselves against the white-robed guests.

Dancing created much merriment for a time, the couples trying to discover each other's identity, and having all they could do to manage their flowing drapery. In the rest time the folding doors suddenly flew open, and a strange sight presented itself. The room beyond was inky black except for the red light burning before a little tent. (Red fire burning in a tin pan; can be bought at any fireworks dealer's.) The tent was open, and inside it sat a witch, high red hat, broomstick and all. In front of her on the ground was an enormous pumpkin, scooped out and filled with tiny pumpkins, the latter made of cotton covered over with yellow crepe paper and tied with baby ribbon, light green for ladies, dark green for men. The witch chanted out an invitation to us, and we went in in turn and received a little pumpkin, she bestowing each one with muttered incantations.

Then the door shut the witch from view, the lights went up in the drawing room, and we had a hilarious time opening the pumpkins and examining our fortunes. Mine had a pair of tiny doll overshoes, and the verse:

"Your hands will play the typewriter and your dainty
    feet
  Will daily need protection from the rain and slush
    and sleet."

The hostess said that with a little ingenuity any number of these verses and favors could be made. Some of the funniest were these:

A tiny United States flag for a lady:

"You will be the president's wife,
    And in Washington lead a gay life."

A thimble for a lady:

"Whether in single or married bliss,
    Sewing's your fortune—so please take this."

A little bunch of scarlet silk floss tied with a blue ribbon, for a man:

"This tress was cut from the dainty head
    Of the very lady you will wed."

A penny for a man:

"Listen well to the words of the witch:
'Earn plenty of money and you'll be rich.'"

A brass button for a man:

"You'll both a soldier and sailor be,
And gallantly fight on the dark blue sea."

After the fortunes were all examined we were conducted once more to the dressing rooms and the sheets and other draperies removed, and then we went in to supper. This was a bounteous feast of the good things of the season: the fall fruits, popcorn, gingerbread and cider. A wooden bowl of nuts was placed at each plate, with a pair of crackers convenient. Suddenly there was a little shriek of surprise; one girl had opened an English walnut and found, instead of a kernel, one of the funny and uncanny worms which the Japanese cut out of vegetable ivory. They are wriggly things, and the shock was great. Most of the nuts were normal, but there were enough bewitched ones to keep the excitement high. One had a tiny black doll not an inch long; some had bits of candy; some brass rings with glass stones. These nuts were all English walnuts, and the hostess told me she had carefully cut them in half with a sharp knife, removed the kernel, put in the prize, and glued the shells together again so that the opening could not be detected.

Finally I got a nut with nothing but a bit of folded paper in it. On it was written: "Don't tell the others." Then came some queer characters which I decided to be words written backward, and when I slipped quietly off to the mirror in the dressing room I made them out to be: "Go on the midnight stroke and dig under the piano for a mighty prize." The backward writing is done this way: Lay a carbon paper on the table duplicating side up, then two pieces of thin white paper on top and write with a hard pencil on the top piece. This will leave the words written backward on the under paper.

It was still half an hour before midnight, and I kept wondering how I was to dig under the piano. I carefully examined the spot specified, without saying anything about it, but thought it unwise to call for a spade and go to work on the hard wood floor.

We played all the time-honored Halloween games and tricks, and all the time I was thinking but could come to no conclusion. As the clock struck 12 we were all in the front hall, and what was my surprise to see the whole party rush to the drawing room and to the piano. Every last one had had a paper with the same directions, and each one thought the secret his alone. When the first astonishment was over, we saw that a number of little pails and shovels had been placed on a white cloth spread beneath the piano, and amid the laughter and good-natured pushing we crept under and dug our prizes out of the soft sand. They were all just alike, favors to take home—paper bonbonnieres shaped like pumpkins.

Soon after we were on our way home, voting the party the very liveliest and best we had ever attended.

A REAL HALLOWEEN

If possible, hold the Halloween festivities in a barn or large kitchen, in the latter case setting the table and having certain of the games there. On All Saints' day, two hundred years ago, every household built its bonfire at nightfall. They made a girdle of flame about the hills of Scotland. Indoors the house was lighted by torches and lanterns till midnight, when the fairies were supposed to be abroad. Strange methods of divination were resorted to by young and old.

Keep constantly in mind that the ancient object of the day was the peering into the future. If possible, have a bonfire. Material may be hoarded a few weeks ahead. Set a few small boys to the blissful job of piling on fresh fuel. Deck the walls of the barn or kitchen with branches of spruce and pine, and among them hang on strong wire rods a splendid array of jack-o'-lanterns or pumpkin lanterns. If possible, contrive somewhere about the house a dimly-lit cozy corner or impromptu booth where a woman versed in palmistry may tell of the future and hint at the past. In every fireplace light a crackling wood fire, and in the kitchen have ready the properties necessary for a real Halloween: baskets of apples, balls of yarn, corn ready for the popper, and a hoard of nuts.

There are so many time-honored games for Halloween that they can scarcely be crowded into one evening's entertainment. Nobody knows how ancient is the game of bobbing for apples, but it certainly never grows old.

Fill a tub nearly to the brim with water and into it put a dozen ruddy apples. Place in the heart of four apples a ring, a ten-cent piece, a thimble and a button. Replace neatly the apple cube which has been cut out for this admission, and the enthusiasm of the bobbers will be heartier with the knowledge of the lottery. The game may be varied for the other guests by holding a fork between the teeth, clasping the hands behind the back, trying to pierce an apple by dropping the fork. Apples may be utilized in another way by tying one to a string, hanging it in a doorway, and still with the hands behind the back trying to take a bite from it. It is so difficult a "stunt" that it is safe to offer a few prizes to the guests who succeed. Long apple parings tossed over the shoulder generally will curl into some shape which predicts the initials of the future lover.

Imagination has full play when the girls search for the profession of the man they will marry by gazing at the white of an egg dropped in a glass of water. The egg will take very queer forms, and it is not hard to picture a ship, a church, an easel, a railroad train, a bridge, or a printing press. There is the perilous custom of following through a dark cellar a ball of yarn, which will lead to somebody's lover. The end may be satisfying enough to make up for the trip. In a room as dark as twilight, a girl may comb her hair and eat an apple before a mirror with a sweet certainty that out of the darkness will steal a reflection of the man she loves.

The young men can name and roast chestnuts for the girls around whom fancy hovers. If a chestnut should explode and jump from the hot coals, that girl had better be left to single blessedness: it is the girl whose chestnut roasts quietly and steadily who will make married life harmonious. If a sufficient number of cabbage stalks can be procured and planted a few days before Halloween, the pulling of them when blindfolded provides a lively half-hour's fun. A "kale stock" is large in prophecy. If it pulls hard, the lover will be hard to win, and courtship and married life may not be wholly happiness; if easily, the future is serene enough. The shape and size of the kale stock prophesy the figure of the future husband or wife, and if there is plenty of earth about the roots it means riches. A candle may be selected and named for as many sweethearts as one possesses—a Halloween guest, maid or man, is supposed to have a lively preference for several. Set the candles lighted in an open window. The one which longest resists the gusts of wind denotes the lover who till death will remain faithful. The Scotch test called "luggies" is a favorite in all Halloween games. Beside the hearth are placed three basins; one has clean water in it, another muddy water, the third is empty. The youths who would know their fate are led blindfolded to the table groping for the basin, dipping their hands in the first one they reach. If it is the clean water, the future bride or groom will be young and handsome; the muddy water tells of a wedding with a widow or widower, none too youthful or attractive; the empty basin foretells single blessedness.

The American palate takes none too kindly to

haggis, sowens, cock-a-leekie or oat cake, so a good substitute would be a hearty country supper served around
the kitchen table. The fall fruits will provide a centerpiece of rare coloring. Cut a great pumpkin into basket
shape and scoop out the inside. Into the shell heap rosy
apples, green and purple grapes, pears, oranges and
bananas. One may choose an excellent menu from
brown bread and baked beans, cold turkey, chicken pie,
fried sausages with hot buckwheats, head cheese, cold
ham or corned beef hash for a first course. Pumpkin
pie, apple pie, doughnuts, waffles and maple syrup, baked
apples and cream, old-fashioned raised cake, gingerbread,
cookies or some puddings, such as brown betty or pan
dowdy, will fill in the sweet course. Cider and coffee
would be suitable for liquid refreshments. Plenty of
nuts served in a wooden chopping bowl may be handed
around with the fruit to "top off with" as in real country hospitality.

The fun of a Halloween entertainment may be
largely enhanced by place cards at the supper table.
These ought of course to deal with games of fortune and
that gazing into the future which belongs to All Saints'
day. The most effective thing would be ragged edged,
rather rough cards. Keep the decorations in strong
black and white effects, using dense India ink as a
medium; it flows admirably from the pen and works
well with a brush. The range of decorations is wide; you
may have witches riding on broomsticks, the black cat,
blinking owls or flitting bats, four-leaved clovers, wish-
bones or the new moon for luck—indeed, anything that

signifies portents and fortune, whether good or bad. A quotation adds largely to the merit of the occasion. To save searching, a number of quotations are here appended suitable for a Halloween party. By the way, Shakespeare will be found rich in sayings of weird and ghostlike nature; Macbeth, Hamlet, and Romeo and Juliet being especially good hunting grounds. Here are some culled from various sources:

"The iron tongue of midnight hath told twelve."

"If you had any eye behind you, you might see more detraction at your heels than fortunes before you."

"I can call spirits from the vasty deep."

"If you can look into the seeds of time,
And say which grain will grow and which will not."

"It was the owl that shrieked, the fatal bellman
Which gives the stern'st good-night."

"There's husbandry in heaven,
Their candles are all out."

"There are more things in heaven and earth, Horatio,
Than are dreamt of in your philosophy."

"No witch hath power to charm,
So hallowed and so gracious is this time."

"How now, you secret, black and midnight hags,
  What is't you do?"

"Show his eyes and grieve his heart,
  Come like shadows, so depart."

"The owl, for all his feathers, was acold."

"The bat takes airy rounds on leathern wings,
  And the hoarse owl his woful dirges sings."

" 'Tis the witching hour of night,
    And the stars they glisten, glisten
    Seeming with bright eyes to listen.
        For what listen they?"

"A farmer traveling with his load,
  Picked up a horseshoe on the road,
  And nailed it fast to his barn door
  That luck might down upon him pour."

"Some there be that shadows kiss;
  Such have but a shadow's bliss."

"Some have mistaken blocks and posts
  For specters, apparitions, ghosts,
    With saucer eyes and horns."

"O heavens, that one might read the book of fate
  And see the revolutions of the times."

"Oh, could we lift the future's sable shroud!"

"Fortune is merry,
  And in this mood will give us anything."

" 'Tis the sunset of life gives me mystical lore,
  And coming events cast their shadows before."

"This day we fashion Destiny, our web of Fate we spin."

"Who can answer where any road leads to?"

> "There swims no goose so gray
>   But soon or late
> She finds some honest gander
>   For her mate."

"This is the fairy land, O spite of spites,
  We talk with goblins, owls and elvish sprites."

A HALLOWEEN COBWEB PARTY

By M. D

A Philadelphia girl had an inspiration for her October 31 party. This was a cobweb party, changed to fit the requirements of Halloween. She took cords of different shades and colors, one for each guest, and wound them over furniture, doorways, et cetera, through the different rooms on the lower floor. At one end of each string she tied an envelope containing a "fortune." The red, yellow and brown cords, with all the varying tints of these colors, had fortunes for the men, while white, blue and green, turquoise, emerald and the like denoted the envelopes for the girls. All cords began in the drawing room, where each fortune hunter selected his or her own according to fancy. Although the cords were never knotted or tied in any way, the maze and tangle was so dense at times that the sport of the evening lasted a good two hours. No one was allowed to touch the fate thread of another player. This regulation added greatly to the difficulty and the fun. The fortunes were concocted in the fertile brain of the hostess. When all the envelopes had been discovered the young people assembled and the prophecies were read aloud. An amusing little trick was perpetrated by the girls upon the men. One of the girls appeared in the parlor costumed as a gypsy and offered with much ceremony to tell each young man the name of his future helpmate. She dealt out cards or shook the grounds in a teacup, making many calculations which meant nothing whatever and asking various questions. Each man in turn received a sealed envelope which he was warned not to open until the fortune telling was over. When the envelope was finally opened each man found his own name upon a card preceded by the word "Mrs."

HALLOWEEN SALAD (Page 250)

SUGGESTIONS FOR HALLOWEEN

By Hester Price

The fireplace and mantel are attractively decorated with products of the field. The first step toward dressing the mantelpiece is to get a board the size of the shelf in order that hammer and tacks may be used with impunity; after this it is a simple matter to arrange the fringe of corn. In the center of the space over the mantelpiece is the silhouette of an owl. Anyone with the least skill in drawing could draw the outline of an owl on water color paper and tint it with brown water color paint. The candle shades are clever imitations of jack-o'-lanterns made of orange colored crepe paper, with eyes, nose and mouth of tissue paper.

An appropriate centerpiece for the Halloween supper table may consist of small papier mache jack-o'-lanterns and splendid chrysanthemums arranged alternately around a mammoth pumpkin carved into a basket. The basket is filled with the shells of mandarin oranges, and is passed to the guests. Each shell contains an article—a penny, a heart, a bachelor's button, tiny china cat, etc., etc. These are supposed to carry a meaning prophetic of the recipient's future.

For the salad, take a fine, large white head of cabbage, cut out the center and cut the sides into decided points. With cloves make eyes, nose and mouth on each side. Fill the center of the cabbage with nut and apple salad. Serve on a large platter garnished with lettuce leaves.

Fill with a mixture of two cups of celery cut fine, one dozen walnut meats blanched and chopped fine, the grated rind of one orange and one cup of tart apples cut in dice, with mayonnaise dressing colored green. Garnish with a tomato cut to look like a rose.

Chestnut Burs—Two ounces of chocolate, four eggs, one-half cup of milk, one teaspoon of vanilla, one-half cup of butter, one and one-half cups of sugar, one heaping teaspoon of baking powder, one and three-fourths cups of flour. Dissolve the chocolate in five tablespoons of boiling water. Beat the butter to a cream, gradually add the sugar, beating all the while; add the yolks, beat again, add the milk, then the melted chocolate and flour. Give the whole a vigorous beating. Beat the whites of the eggs to a stiff froth, stir them carefully into the mixture, add the vanilla and baking powder. Mix quickly and lightly, turn into a square buttered cake pan, bake in a moderate oven forty-five minutes. When

A MANTEL DECORATED FOR HALLOWEEN

cold cut into squares with a sharp knife, trim squares into balls, roll balls in icing colored a delicate green, then in grated cocoanut colored green, and pile them on a platter or in a cake basket. The cocoanut is easily colored by tinting about three tablespoons of water a good green with vegetable coloring paste. Mix in the cocoanut, spread on a large platter to dry before using on the cakes.

Chestnut Parfait in Apple Shells—Select bright red apples of medium and uniform size, cut off the tops, scoop out the inside carefully with a silver spoon, notch the edges with a silver knife and put the prepared shells in cold water until ready to serve.

Chestnut Parfait—Beat yolks of eight eggs until light, add one cup of maple syrup. Place the mixture on a slow fire until the eggs have thickened enough to make a deep coating on the spoon. Turn it into a bowl and beat it with a whip until cold; it will then be very light. Add a teaspoonful of vanilla to the custard when it is taken from the fire. When the custard is cold add a pint of cream whipped to a stiff froth. If any liquid has drained from the cream, do not let it go in. When this is ready to go in the freezer, add a cup of boiled chestnuts cut in dice. Roll in powdered sugar, so each piece will be dry and separate and not sink to the bottom. Stir in quickly and pack the freezer immediately in ice and salt for three hours. Serve in apple shells.

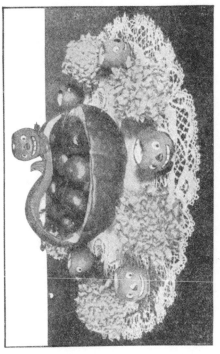

A HALLOWEEN CENTERPIECE

HOLIDAY FESTIVITIES

HOLIDAY FESTIVITIES

A SPELLING BEE

By Mrs. Dan Hon

THANKSGIVING morning some club women in Arkansas sent their friends invitations to an old-time supper and spelling bee. Each guest was presented with a dainty card, tied with pink and green, the club colors, bearing the best wishes of "ye hostesses." The bill of fare consisted of turkey, 'possum, salad, pickles, jelly, mince pie, fruit, cake and coffee. Supper was served early. Appropriate centerpieces were made for each of the three tables of pumpkins cut in halves and polished, and then by the aid of a sharp knife the edges were scalloped and each ridge was carved in tiny sprays of flowers. The baskets thus formed were each placed on a mat of crinkled tissue paper, and filled to overflowing with oranges, rosy-cheeked apples and grapes. Candles were used to light the tables.

After supper, someone was selected to act the part of "Squire Hawkins," while two more "chose up." The words were dictated from Webster's spelling book, better known as the "blue back," and spelled according to the old-time method. The first prize was a "blue back" spelling book, while a dunce cap and a bag of peppermint candy were given the one who first misspelled a word. The spelling bee was enjoyed by doctors, lawyers, editors, teachers, merchants, clerks, misses in their teens, matrons, grandmothers, and one great-grandmother.

THE THANKSGIVING TABLE

By Marie Eulalie Moran

To begin with the napery, a cloth patterned with leaves, chrysanthemums or nut burs is most desirable for this festival, but one with a snowdrop or other unobtrusive geometrical design may be used with good effect. Then comes the question of the centerpiece, whether it shall be fruit or flowers. Both possess charming decorative possibilities, but sentiment and a taste for symbolism will decide in favor of the fruit in many homes.

The description of two centerpieces planned by clever women for their tables on Thanksgiving day will probably be welcomed by the housewives who are seeking suggestions for the novel arrangement of fruit. The first woman, who is an artist and spends her vacations in the mountains, has made a low, oval-shaped basket of pine cones with a wide arched willow handle to hold her fruit. A wreath of glowing red bittersweet will encircle the basket, and a length of the vine and a cluster of thistle puff balls will adorn the handle. The second woman has made a cornucopia of plaited grass. She is going to have brightly tinted vines and dusky berries around it, and have its wealth of autumn fruits spill out upon the table. Either of these designs is a charming centerpiece; so is a large Indian canoe piled high with fruits, with the grapes and vines hanging over its sides. This canoe may be woven of grass or be made of bark or leaves.

If flowers are to decorate the table, choose them from the hardy varieties of the season. The chrysanthemum, of course, heads the list. Any scheme of color may be carried out with the aid of this flower, which offers the decorator snowy white, pale sulphur and brilliant yellow, all the shades of bronze and red, delicate lilac and pink blooms, in clusters or feathery pompons, or tightly curled balls. But unless willing to have a tall centerpiece, put the vases of chrysanthemums at the corners of the table, or use another flower; these proud blossoms are sorry objects when arranged in a low, compact mound; they are then as characterless and unlovely as a crinkled paper mat. Cosmos, roses or carnations are also appropriate, and the autumn grains, berries and leaves.

For the guest cards and dinner favors there are many quaint and dainty devices. Cards cut out and painted to represent the fall fruits or vegetables and lettered in gold are very attractive. These cut-out shapes are pasted on the tops of small boxes of bonbons for souvenirs. A very droll little favor is a round box of candy beans, the top ornamented with a Puritan hat. The hats are made of black paper and are pasted on the box tops—they should be the exact size of the box. Letter "Thanksgiving," and the year, around the hat brim in gold. A little practice and experiment will enable one to become expert at making these little hats. Deftness is required in rolling up the tall crown and pasting it neatly. When dry, it is joined to the wide brim and a cord is tied around it. Any picture illustrating the Puritan costume will be a sufficient guide in making them.

When cake is a part of the Thanksgiving dinner, give your guests a surprise by serving it as a pumpkin or turkey. A firm cake a day old should be used, so it will not break in modeling. The easiest way of making the pumpkin is to bake the cake in two fluted pans, and when cool join them together in the center with jelly, taking care to join the flutes exactly. Then with a brush coat the entire cake with jelly, dust with sugar and let dry. Ice with almond paste or cream fondant, melted as for dipping candy. This icing is colored orange. Insert a stem and leaves in the pumpkin. Or a large cake may be built up tall and modeled with a sharp knife into pumpkin shape and then iced. Orange marmalade is a nice filling for this cake. For the turkey a large square loaf or layer cake is needed. With a knife model it to look as much like a roast turkey as possible. Icing the turkey is a very particular piece of work. For the light tints, mix saffron and caramel colorings with the white icing and then shade Mr. Turkey up with caramel to make his skin look crisp and brown. If the plain dark caramel is too dull a brown, add a few drops of red and saffron to brighten it. While the icing is still soft, take a coarse-meshed wire strainer and press all over it to imitate the grain of the turkey's skin. Two sticks of candy are then put in the cake legs for bones, and frills of white paper tied around them with ribbons. Parsley may be used as a garnish if intense realism is desired.

A BACHELOR'S THANKSGIVING DINNER

By Hester Price

It seems only fair that someone should take the trouble to plan a suitable Thanksgiving dinner for those men who are thrown upon their own resources on the day that one always associates with family gatherings, a dinner equally available, too, for families. In getting the desired effect, much will depend upon the quality and the proper laying of the cloth. An ideal bachelor's dinner is elegant, but rather severe in appointments. Handsome damask gives elegance to a table, even when the decoration is very simple. Yellow color effects are always satisfactory, and they are particularly brilliant when used with artificial light. The chrysanthemum is the king of November flowers. It is astonishing how decorative even a few of these splendid Japanese blossoms are. Use a flat silver bowl filled with yellow chrysanthemums for a centerpiece. Light the dining room and table with clear wax candles shaded with candle shades made of artificial chrysanthemums. The menu should be a skillful combination of what may be termed the national dishes with others especially liked by men, and above all do not neglect the brown November nut.

CHESTNUT BOULETTES

MENU

Oyster cocktail

Oxtail soup

Young turkey   Cranberry jelly

Chestnut boulettes   Baked tomatoes

Mashed potatoes

Olives   Salted nuts   Radishes

Sweetbreads with Madeira in chafing-dish

Lettuce salad with French dressing

Cheese croquettes   Pastry strips

Pumpkin fanchonettes

Orange ice

Old-fashioned hickory nut cakes

Black coffee

Roasted chestnuts

FOR MAKING THE COFFEE AT TABLE

After the soup is removed, the butler should pass a tray on which are numbered tickets. Each guest takes one. Immediately the turkey is brought in "decorated" with corresponding tickets, each cut being numbered. This is an unusual "turkey raffle," and the matching of numbers is sure to occasion a great deal of interest and amusement.

The introduction of the chafing-dish to prepare the entree would give to this jolly little dinner an air of *bon-camaraderie,* provided the host is a clever manipulator of it. The chafing-dish is often tricky, and one needs to guard well against failure or awkward delay. The fanchonette or individual pumpkin pie is a convenient way in which to present an old friend under a new name. The recipe for the orange ice is an exceptionally delicious one. It is attractively served in paper ice cups covered with artificial flowers. At any dinner the demi-tasse of coffee should be so perfect as to leave nothing to be desired. Many men take pride in preparing such a cup of coffee at the table. To make a successful cup of coffee only a few short rules need be observed. First secure an up to-date coffee pot, planned to make drip coffee. Science says never boil coffee. Use pulverized coffee and freshly boiling water. Here are some of the recipes used in the menu:

Salted Nuts—A mixture of almonds, filberts and walnuts salted is a good combination. The filberts are blanched, as are the almonds, but the skin is not removed from the walnuts.

Orange Ice—Put one pint of water and one and one-half cups of sugar on to boil; chip the yellow rind of three oranges, add to the syrup, boil five minutes, and stand away to cool. Peel eight nice, juicy oranges and one lemon, cut them in halves, take out the seeds and squeeze out all the juice; mix with the syrup, strain through a cloth and freeze. It may be necessary to add a little sugar. This will depend upon the sweetness of the oranges.

PASTRY STRIPS

Cheese Croquettes—One cup grated cheese, whites of four eggs beaten to a stiff froth, pinch of red pepper, two drops of Worcestershire sauce. Mix cheese and whites of eggs, beat well. Make into shapes, roll in bread crumbs and let stand for an hour or two in a cold place. Fry them just before serving.

Sweetbreads with Fresh Mushrooms—Wash well two pairs of sweetbreads. Put them in boiling water,

THE TURKEY NUMBERED FOR THE "RAFFLE"

add one bay leaf, a sprig of parsley, a teaspoon of salt
and one-fourth teaspoon of pepper; cover and simmer
for thirty minutes, then throw them into cold water,
changing the water to cool them quickly. When the
sweetbreads are cold pick them in small pieces, rejecting
all skin. Drain them free from water and put in a
bowl. Now peel two pounds of meadow mushrooms,
cut them with a silver knife into quarters and throw into
a bowl of cold water. Make one-fourth pound of butter
into four balls, put one-half of it into the chafing-dish;
when melted drain the mushrooms, put them into the
hot butter, cover and cook very slowly for ten minutes;
add the sweetbreads, cover again for ten minutes; then
add one-half pint of thick cream, the remainder of the
butter, a teaspoon of salt, one-half teaspoon of white
pepper; stir carefully until hot; add four tablespoons
of Madeira wine and serve. It is hardly necessary to
say that the sweetbreads and mushrooms are only
creamed at the table, the entire preparation being made
previously in the kitchen.

Chestnut Boulettes—Mix one cup of mashed chestnuts, two egg yolks beaten slightly, two tablespoons of
cream, one tablespoon of sugar, one-eighth teaspoon of
salt, one teaspoon of sherry. When cool fold in whites
of two eggs beaten stiff, form into small balls, crumb,
egg, crumb again, fry in hot fat.

Pumpkin Fanchonettes—Mix one and one-half cups
of stewed pumpkin very dry, with two cups of milk, one
beaten egg, a large half cup of brown sugar, one teaspoon of cinnamon, one-half teaspoon each of salt and

ginger. Line individual tins with pastry and bake in a slow oven until brown on top.

Old-Fashioned Hickory Nut Cake—Of all the nut cakes there is none better than this old-fashioned one. Cream together one and one-half cups of fine granulated or pulverized sugar and one-half cup of butter. Add three-fourths of a cup of sweet milk, two and one-half cups of flour sifted with two teaspoons of baking powder and one cup of hickory nut meats dredged lightly with flour. Lastly add one-half teaspoon of vanilla and fold in the whites of four eggs beaten to a stiff froth.

A JEST CHRISTMAS TREE

By Belle Aubry

Decorate the tree fancifully and then confine all gifts to those costing five or ten cents, either purchased outright or made at the inspiration of a merry fancy. Each present should have some gayety-provoking reference to the vocation, avocation or fad of the recipient, but the "hits" must be good-humored. To wound the feelings of a guest even in jest is unpardonable.

The invitation to such a party might run in this wise: "Dear Mrs. Farnham, Santa Claus has sent us word that much to his regret he will not be able to be with us on Christmas eve, owing to pressing engagements elsewhere. Will not you and Mr. Farnham make up for this disappointment by spending Christmas eve with us? We are asking a few other friends from eight to twelve, and upon each and every one is laid the embargo to come empty-handed. May we count upon the pleasure of seeing you both? Believe me, faithfully yours, Helen Macy Vedder." The item about the embargo shows that you do not wish presents, which a Christmas time invitation otherwise is taken to mean by many people. The notes should be sent at least ten days ahead, as Christmas week teems with engagements.

The pivot of success for this jest tree is the spokesman. He must be selected with much thought, and should be someone who knows all the guests well, has a nimble wit, ready tongue and will take his office so much to heart that he will make a point of being amusing in his remarks as he presents the presents; these will be suggestive in themselves, and he must familiarize himself with the whole situation of course beforehand. If this master of the tree ceremonies can be the host, so much the better.

It is not witty or kind to give a mirror to a girl known to be vain, but it raises a laugh without a sting to present a girl baby doll to the mother of a family all of boys. A wreath of laurel for the young singer is a pretty bit of sentiment, and even a package of Chinese incense sticks will please the studio-dwelling artist. The stern man can but laugh over a gay red stocking filled with sweets, and the crack shot of the rifle team over a toy gun, and the divinity student over a toy church. These veriest trifles did duty among others last Christmas to delight the guests at a five-cent gift tree given for its oddity in a beautiful New York home on Fifth

avenue to amuse guests in evening dress and in the habit
of giving and receiving gifts of much money value.

It is much more enjoyable to limit the number of
guests to those who can sit at table for the spread.   A
buffet, stand-up or lap-supported supper is forgivable
only when the company is of necessity large, as at a
wedding, and the numbers and ability of the waiters
commensurate.

One appetizing supper menu that is not difficult to
make ready or expensive, consists of creamed oysters
served in small rolls hollowed out, salted almonds,
chicken salad, water or cream ices, bonbons, cake and
punch.   Everything but the oysters and coffee can be
prepared beforehand, and these take only a short time
at the last minute.   But the ices require skillful and
timely service, and unless there is competent domestic
service to wait on the table, substitute fruit jellies with
whipped cream for the ices, and have everything on
the table.

When the oysters cannot be had, sweetbreads can be
substituted; chicken and mushrooms in cream sauce
are another substitute.   These creamed dishes, lobster
a la Newburg, and many similar conceits may be prepared on the table in the presence of the guests if one is
accomplished in the use of the chafing-dish so that she
can feel at ease and talk as she works.   The chafing-
dish must be large, or there must be more than one when
there are several guests.

An appetizing little supper where chafing-dishes do
not seem to be in harmony with the circumstances can

be made from a large and delicious chicken pie, flanked by cold ham and turkey with relishes, preserved fruit served with thick sweet cream, cake and coffee. There should always be a punch bowl full of lemonade convenient of access throughout the evening.

The charm of hospitality does not lie in concocting dishes so marvelous to look at that they invite the camera's attention (and make one wonder just how many times each viand was handled before it finally arrived at its place in the resulting puzzle). The charm of hospitality is the art of doing what is done, not in the number or extent of things done, in the atmosphere of good cheer and the genuineness of the welcome, not in any suggested bulletin of expenditures.

A TWENTIETH-CENTURY CHRISTMAS TREE

By Alice Chittenden

A very respectable winter landscape can be evolved with a few chairs and stools of uneven hight, some old sheets and cotton batting. Arrange this "furniture landscape" behind the tree, throw the sheets over to produce a hilly effect, wrinkle them into the form of snowdrifts, and pin tufts of cotton batting upon the cloth, picking it out into fluffy masses. Fix the tree firmly to a standard, which should be screwed to the floor, as absolute rigidity is essential. Arrange more muslin and cotton into irregular piles of snow under and in front of the tree and fasten little tufts of cotton lightly here and there in the crotches formed by the branches. After the tree is completely trimmed, simulate the sparkle of new-fallen snow under artificial light by powdering the cotton with fine isinglass, and when the tapers are lighted the effect will be really magical. The larger branches, if brushed over at the last with thin mucilage and strewn thickly with fine salt, will have the appearance of glistening frost.

To produce a moonlight effect, dress the tree in white and silver, hanging it with white and silver glass balls, diamond dusted popcorn garlands and snowballs. One of the latter should be provided for each child. Fashion a number of cube-shaped boxes from stiff writing paper, fill with candies or with the smaller gifts and wrap into a round ball with loosely picked batting, tying with fine white spool thread to keep the shape, and with a crochet hook pulling the cotton from under the thread so as to hide the latter and make a fluffy ball. Yellow and gold is a pretty color for decoration, which can be carried out with gilded popcorn and nuts, yellow candles, yellow glass balls and gifts wrapped in yellow tissue paper with ornaments of the same material.

Encourage the youngest child to help in the dressing of the tree. The tawdry, pudgy little ornaments their baby fingers have fashioned are more wonderful in their eyes than the most costly ones you can purchase. After the trimming is complete, banish them from the room and hang on the presents, and there will still be a surprise in store for them. If the Christmas tree has any place in the moral universe, it is when trimmed not only for, but by, the children.

For a Sunday school or "settlement" Christmas celebration, a "Christmas cave" gives scope for originality and striking scenic effects. Build a cave-shaped box on a raised platform, drape inside and out with white muslin, fasten evergreen boughs about the entrance and at the back, draping all of these with loose tufts of cotton like new-fallen snow, and sprinkling them with mica. Sprays of red berries can be introduced with splendid effect. White covered steps must lead up to the cave, about the mouth of which may be spread white fur rugs. Let the candles be fastened plentifully around the cave, but leave the rest of the room very dimly lighted. Dress a pretty, golden-haired little girl as a fairy with wings and spangles to enter the cave and bring out the gifts, and a couple of little boys as imps or brownies to deliver them. Low music should be played in some concealed corner, with now and again a song or chorus by a band of children dressed as fairies.

People cannot be too careful in guarding against fire when trimming a Christmas tree. There have been scores of Christmas tree fatalities in homes and in Sunday schools which a little care might have prevented. The present writer once set a tree in a blaze, consuming nearly half of it, tinsel ornaments going with the green branches. A tiny candle had been wired too high and it took only a few minutes of its brisk heat to char a branch above it and start a flame. A thick portiere was torn from its pole and thrown over the blaze. If it had not been at hand the light window curtains in another minute would have caught fire. Since that Christmas our tree has always been placed in the center of the room, and we have eschewed cotton wool, tissue paper angels and celluloid ornaments. First of all, we wire each candle securely in place at the farthest end of a branch which has nothing above it, either fir tree or trimming. Then as the tree is denuded we watch carefully the fast disappearing candles. Sometimes one of them, nearly burned down, will topple over or be merely a spark of flame, but near to something inflammable, will be a menace.

AN INNOVATION

By Anne Warner

The housemother was "raised" on historic ground and had no thought other than to serve the regulation Thanksgiving dinner, till a certain little girl thus expressed her sentiments about a week before the day set aside for praise and gluttony—to be followed by a week of indigestion and prayer: "Mamma," she said, "I can't be thankful on Thanksgiving if we are going to have a great big dinner, and I'm going to feel *all body* as I did last year. I'm sick of turkey, anyway!" Furthermore, the housemother overheard remarks by another member of her flock to the effect that it is hard lines holidays when a whole family lives in a city—and the same city, at that—and when not one of them is considerate enough to own a farm for the sole purpose of having the traditional place for reunions.

This set the housemother to wondering if she could not at least introduce an element of surprise by changing the time-honored menu, and from that to planning to make the maligned city dining room suggest harvest season in the country. These ideas bore fruit—or rather vegetables—and when the project was finally carried out, the result justified the wearying search after the "common things" that made the room give one almost the feeling one has out-of-doors in autumn

"When the mist is on the cornfield,
And the sun is droppin' slow."

Tall sheaves of tasseled corn, still bearing shining red and yellow ears, rustled in the corners and shimmered round the cheery fireplace. Masses of swaying wheat and nodding oats, combined with vegetables— few of us realize that many of these are beautiful as well as useful—formed groups of brilliant color wherever in the room they could be arranged without suggesting a greengrocer's shop, a plate rail near the ceiling lending itself most amiably to the scheme. In the center of the dining room was a large mirror mat. Upon this were heaped the fruits that our New England climate flavors as no other can. Care was taken to mound the fruit to give it hight and stability at the same time. The housemother thinks that the intervals of a dinner can be more profitably and pleasantly filled in otherwise than by chasing truant bits of fruit that become dislodged from the centerpiece and roll out, threatening to cause the collapse of the elaborate structure. The menu was a queer mingling of the old and the new in cookery —but here it is:

Canape Lorenzo
(Chamberlin)

Roast "spar'rib"   Apple sauce
Stuffed onions   Potato roses
Cider

Chicken pie   Cauliflower au gratin
Celery   Cranberry jelly
Indian pudding, sauce   Grilled nuts
New century sandwiches   Cream peppermints
Coffee

Canape Lorenzo—Chop a small shallot, fry lightly in two ounces of butter, without coloring. Add a tablespoonful of flour wet with a pint of cream, then one pint of crab meat; salt and pepper to taste and leave on the fire till it bubbles. Cut slices of bread one-quarter of an inch thick, trim in any desired shape and toast on one side only. Put the mixture on the toasted side and cover one-eighth of an inch thick with butter prepared as follows: One-quarter of a pound of butter, one-half a pound of grated Parmesan cheese and a seasoning of both red and white pepper. Lay the canapes on a buttered dish and color in the oven.

For the roast, select carefully the loin and ribs of a "beastie" both fresh and young. Plunge this cut quickly into scalding water; wipe and rub with salt, pepper, sage and flour. Bake in a moderately hot oven twenty or even twenty-five minutes to the pound, with a small quantity of water in the pan. It is more wholesome partly or entirely cold, so can be cooked early. Serve the roses on the same platter with it, as a garnish. To two cupfuls of seasoned mashed potatoes add the yolks of two eggs and white of one, and beat. Put in a pastry bag, and as it is pressed through the tube guide it first in a circle, then irregularly wind it round till it comes to a point in the center. The little piles of potato will look like roses—if you are imaginative. Brush them over lightly with egg, put a bit of butter on each and brown slightly in the oven.

The housemother does not believe in spoiling apple sauce with overmuch seasoning and cooking. Use a graniteware or porcelain kettle. Have in readiness freshly boiling water; a good fire; the sugar, measured; and selected Baldwin apples, large, unblemished and warm. Allow from one-half to three-quarters of a cup of granulated sugar to eight apples—the exact quantity depending upon the development of the sweet tooth in the family. Pare and quarter the fruit with all haste, laying the pieces in the kettle core side down; sprinkle over the sugar, pour on about three cups of boiling water, cover the kettle with a close-fitting lid and cook over a quick fire only until the apple quarters are partly transparent. Slip the contents of the kettle into a shallow earthen dish *at once,* keeping them right side up in the transfer, and put the dish in a cool, airy place. The sauce will be white and "sightly" and taste of apple.

Stuffed Spanish Onions—Peel the onions under water and scoop out from the top a portion of the center. Parboil five minutes and turn upside down to drain. Make a stuffing of the chopped onion taken from the centers, softened bread crumbs, salt, pepper and a generous amount of butter. Fill the onions heaping full and sprinkle the top with buttered crumbs. Cover and cook till tender (about an hour) in a pan containing a small quantity of water. Let them brown a very little before taking from the oven.

Just a few points as to the pie! Make it big, in consideration for the children and the pork-prejudiced. In preparing the chickens take out the oysters and discard the rest of the back with the legs and the tips of the wings; a pie is no place for these. Season the gravy highly, thicken it also and prepare more than the immediate need demands, for use when warming the left-over portion. Make the paste like baking-powder biscuit dough, only richer; both little and big can indulge to the extent of capacity then. In the "good old times" the partaker ate chicken pie crust with dyspeptic dreams imminent; and no wonder, with a pound of butter in an under crust and two pounds in the upper! Use a flaring baking dish and line sides only. When chicken is snugly packed in, and gravy containing a pinch of curry poured over, cover with paste having a circular opening *cut out of it*, not cut and turned back. Edge the pie with a border of twisted dough.

Old-fashioned Cranberry Jelly—To every quart of

cranberries allow one cup of boiling water and one-half a cup of seeded raisins which have been boiled in a little water for three-quarters of an hour. Cover and cook soft over a quick fire. Rub through a colander and return to the saucepan. Add one pint of sugar and simmer five minutes, stirring constantly. Pour into crockery molds. For sauce, allow one pint of water instead of a cup, and do not strain it; or, if preferred, make a sugar syrup, then add cranberries and raisins and cook tender.

Cauliflower au Gratin—Cauliflower should be creamy white without black spots. Pick off the outside leaves, invert and soak in cold salted water for an hour. Tie in a bag and cook in boiling salted water for about twenty minutes, or till tender. Drain and break it into flowerets. Put a layer in an Edam cheese shell, cover with cream sauce and alternate layers of cauliflower and sauce till the shell is heaping full. Sprinkle top with buttered bread crumbs and set shell in oven to brown the crumbs. Use a dish if the cheese shell is not at hand.

Indian Pudding—Indian pudding, like several other savory common dishes which depend for digestibility on long cooking, is one for the person who is conscious of a digestive apparatus to be wary of when not under his own vine and fig tree. Get old-fashioned bolted meal, if possible; not that which is usually sold by grocers and which has the keeping qualities and flavor of sawdust. Follow any good recipe for combining proportions of milk, meal, suet, molasses, salt and ginger, with or without eggs, and cook it, covered, in a slow oven for four or five hours. Stir occasionally and add milk if the mixture gets too thick. Next day add more milk and *cook again for the same length of time.* Many like the flavor given if a liberal sprinkling of candied orange peel, or currants, or a layer of quartered apples, is put in the bottom of the baking dish. With Indian pudding the homely sauce of whipped cream mixed with shaved maple sugar "can't be beat," but either hard sauce or caramel is excellent. The pudding at this particular dinner was garnished round about with a row of baked apples, sweet and sour alternating. The sour ones had been cored and the hollows filled with sugar before baking, and all cooked till soft.

Grilled Nuts—Boil two cupfuls of granulated sugar with one-half a cup of water until it hairs. Add two cupfuls of blanched and dried almonds and filberts mixed and stir till the sugar grains and clings to the nuts. When well coated and before they get into one mass turn them out and separate any that have stuck together.

The "sandwiches" were made of big, plump, rich raisins filled with almonds or hickory nuts.

Coffee (the housemother's way)—In a well-scalded and well-aired coffee pot put the same number of heaping tablespoons of coffee as cups to be served. Add as many clean eggshells as cups, or if white of egg is preferred allow one white for clearing three cups. Add one tablespoon of cold water for each cup, and mix. Pour in the requisite number of cups of freshly boiling water and boil five minutes. Pour a little cold water down the spout; stir in one tablespoon of fresh coffee and a pinch of salt and set where it will keep hot, but not simmer, for ten minutes. Fill the nozzle with tissue paper. If there is a delay in serving, at the end of ten minutes pour the coffee from the grounds into a clean coffee pot and keep hot till wanted.

Between dinner and the good-byes, the children amused themselves by etching and inking faces on all the little sugar pumpkins among the decorations. They adorned them further, to their immense satisfaction, by tying and gluing on white tissue paper in the shape of caps with frills and strings. These treasures they carried proudly home. At bedtime, when the housemother went to tuck in the original cause of the innovation (which I shall probably continue to do till she's

twenty-one), she said sleepily: "Mamma, everybody enjoyed this Thanksgiving dinner, because—it wasn't one!" N. B.—If you must celebrate the day by eating turkey, get one from Rhode Island; they are the best. Their title to superiority does not depend upon the fairy story that they are of different breed from the ordinary idiotic barnyard fowl, nor that their daily food consists of chestnuts ground up with porterhouse steak; but simply that, owing to the limited area of the state, they do not toughen muscle or lose flesh from overexercise

OTHER SPECIAL OCCASIONS

OTHER SPECIAL OCCASIONS

A BIRTHDAY PARTY

By Jeannette Young

ON her seventy-second birthday, a dear friend received us with dignity and courtesy. On her silver hair, arranged in side puffs, was a lace cap. Her gray silk gown with its white lace fichu and dainty work bag made her look like an old portrait come to life. Grandma sat in state, and we all passed in line, leaving on her lap our gifts and receiving a kiss in return. Two or three unique features I will tell you of. There were fifty-two letters, each containing a picture of the writer and describing some pleasant incident or pleasure in their life wherein the hostess had shared; one letter to be opened each Sunday morning of the coming year. But the loveliest gift of all was from her six children, nine grandchildren and one wee great-grandchild —a silver rosary composed of silver hearts, each one containing a picture of child, grandchild and wee one; while the large pendant heart held a picture of the grandfather encircled by a lock of white hair. Grandma on the arm of her eldest son preceded us to the supper table, taking her place by the silver tea urn. In the center of the table was a rich fruit birthday cake, made after her own good receipt, garnished with a wreath

of myrtle.   What a delicious old-time supper.   Hot bis-
cuits, fresh butter, boned cold fowls, meats, salads, cakes,
creams, jellies and delicious tea.   Grandma was waited
upon by her two youngest daughters and two eldest
granddaughters.   We had an evening of old-time games,
"forfeits," "spin the platter," making gales of merriment.

VALENTINE CONTESTS

By Mary Dawson

One of the new and pretty ways of opening the
valentine party by a choice of partners for the games of
the evening is the decision of the envelopes, which is
arranged in this way: Take a package of old-fashioned
valentine envelopes, those having embossed design and
long flaps.   Draw or paint on each a different sort of
flower.   Write the name of a certain girl who is to be
present on a card and inclose it in the envelope, form-
ing as many floral envelopes as there are girls in the
party.   Now write the names of all the flowers represented upon separate cards.   Have the name cards in a
basket or dish in the vestibule and the envelopes—sealed,
of course—on the drawing room table.   Each man
coming in selects the flower he prefers from the basket
in the hall.   On entering the drawing room he receives
the envelope decorated with the chosen flower.   When
all guests have arrived the floral envelopes are opened.
The girl whose name is found in the envelope becomes
the partner of the man who chose her emblem.

A HEART PARTY FOR FEBRUARY 14

By Marjorie March

The text of this party is to be simplicity, as it is only one of the many ways that a busy housewife may entertain her friends inexpensiveiy. The invitations should be on white notepaper with perhaps a tiny heart drawn in red ink at the top (Cupid's coat of arms). The hostess herself should dress in white, red, or red and white in combination. The chief expense will be for flowers, but two bunches of carnations will suffice, which, mingled with smilax, will make a centerpiece for both dining room and drawing room table.

A charming cozy corner can easily be arranged for the headquarters of the game by pushing the table with the flowers into one corner; with a divan with sofa cushions, a potted palm or so, and suspended from the ceiling an immense Japanese umbrella to overshadow the table. In fact, for an informal evening where supper is simply to be passed, the more cozy corners, inviting seats and chairs arranged for tete-a-tetes, the better.

The success of entertaining is to start people entertaining themselves. For the game to be played, which is called the game of hearts (though not the popular game of cards), the list cards should have at the top the same little red emblem of love. The game consists of a list of seleeted quotations from poems on love, the players to guess from what poets the quotations are chosen. Pieces of paper and pencils should be provided for all the guests. The hostess, of course, cannot play, as she knows the answers, but takes charge of all the slips of paper as they are returned to her. A prize is given to the one who guesses all the quotations, or the greatest number. But the sequel to the game is perhaps the greatest fun. It is simply a slight change in the old game of word and question. But the words must be chosen from the names of the noted poets, and the question must pertain to love in some shape or manner. Each person writes a word, turns down the paper and passes it to his left-hand neighbor, who in turn writes the question, passing it on likewise. The third person is to write a four-line valentine, bringing in the word and answering the question. A vote is taken afterward as to the best valentine and a prize given. The prizes should be in the shape of a heart, and can be simple, a candy box filled, a stickpin, a pincushion or cut glass dish; any of the countless articles bearing that design. For the first part of the game take such bits of verses as the following, from well-known poets:

"Life and love will soon come by,
There, little girl, don't cry."
—James Whitcomb Riley.

"God's love and peace be with thee
Wheresoe'er this soft autumnal air
Lifts the dark tresses of thy hair."
—John Greenleaf Whittier.

"Love is not love which alters when it alteration finds,
Or bends with the remover to remove."
                              —William Shakespeare.

"True love is but a humble, low-born thing,
  And hath its food served up in earthenware."
                              —James Russell Lowell.

"I take you as a gift that God has given
  And I love you."
                              —Adelaide Anne Proctor.

"I arise from dreams of thee
    And a spirit in my feet
  Has led me—who knows how—
    To thy chamber window, sweet."
                              —Percy Bysshe Shelley.

"And all hearts do pray God love her,
  Ay and always, in good sooth,
  We may all be sure He doth."
                              —Elizabeth Barrett Browning.

"The white rose weeps, she is late,
  The larkspur listens. I hear, I hear,
And the lily whispers, I wait."
                              —Alfred Tennyson.

"Oh, that we two were maying
  Down the stream of the soft spring breeze."
                              —Charles Kingsley.

"Kissing her hair, I sat against her feet,
    Wove and unwove it, wound and found it sweet."
                            —Algernon Charles Swinburne.

"And in that twilight hush. God drew their hearts
    Indissolubly close. For what is love
But his most perfect weaving?"
                            —Lucy Larcom.

"Too full of love my soul is to find place
    Eor fear or anger."
                            —Edwin Arnold.

"It isn't the thing you do, dear,
    It's the thing you leave undone,
Which gives you a bit of a heart-ache
    At the setting of the sun."
                            —Margaret Elizabeth Sangster.

For the second part of the game, I will give one
cr two verses composed at one of these parties. They
must of neeessity be rather absurd, but fun lends itself
easily to their reading: One word written and turned
down was "Burns," from Robert Burns. The question
written below was: "Must your wife know how to
make bread?" The verse that the third person wrote
was:

"Oh, maiden gentle and good-looking,
    I beg to ask, art fond of cooking?
My ardor burns—canst make good bread?
Well-bred—good bread!—wilt thou me wed?"

A second was, the word being "Greenleaf," from John Greenleaf Whittier, the question: "Do you love your sweetheart enough to go shopping with her?"

"Hadst thou asked me to pluck a green leaf from a tree
  When frost claims the earth, 'twere more easy for me,
  Than to think of poor Cupid a-wearied to stopping
  When told to make love to a maiden when shopping! !"

The menu for this entertainment should be most simple: coffee or chocolate and heart-shaped sandwiches, ices and fancy cakes in heart shapes. The viands should all be passed from the dining room table, which should be covered with a spotless white cloth. Candlesticks with white candles and red shades should yield their soft light, and the spicy fragrance of the carnation centerpiece will add to the simple charm.

A WASHINGTON'S BIRTHDAY PARTY

By E. M.

The birthday of George Washington was delightfully celebrated once in a boarding school, where forty girls joined in the fun, all garbed in Martha Washington gowns. Forty pairs of hands had made light work of decorations and party preparations. The affair may be too elaborate to be carried out in full by the ordinary hostess, who must perforce be caterer, decorator and entertainer all in one, still the arrangement can be simplified, the ideas adapted and the party made none the less delightful.

Supper was served in the great dining room, where a round table had been exquisitely linened and artistically adorned. The electric bulbs in the ceiling were swathed in scarlet tissue paper, and between them ran wreaths of smilax, simulating the never-to-be-forgotten red of the cherry and the green of its leaves. More smilax, with milliner's cherries, clipped from cheap artificial wreaths, was draped about pictures, over the sideboards, the doors and the windows. In the center of the round table stood a grand decoration, on which the girls had worked for a week.

It was a low tree, with slender branches. To it had been wired a profusion of leaves cut from stiff green paper, and cherries made from a dab of cotton wool twisted inside a round of scarlet tissue paper. The work was so cleverly done that it would have been hard to imagine the tree and its fruit were not real. The base of the tree was set firmly into a tin plate filled with melted lead, which kept it as steady as if planted in the ground. The leaden base was covered with a wreathing of smilax. It stood within another smilax wreath nearly five feet across, and within the circle was a scattering of green cherry leaves and scarlet cherries, with slender green stems of milliner's wire. Attached to the stems of forty cherries on the tree were narrow ribbons, which alternated in color, green and scarlet. They ran to each plate at the round table and ended in a jaunty bow, through which was passed a silver spoon with the head of the father of our country in relief in the bowl, while on the handle was the date.

The dishes used were in old blue, each service plate bearing a scene from revolutionary history. The place cards were the unique product of one schoolgirl, who had a gift for printing beautifully. Each card, four by five inches in size, was made with a border which looked as if there was an American flag under, with a white card laid upon it. Within this border of red, white and blue was pasted a small fine reproduction of Gilbert Stuart's George Washington, then underneath a sentence from some famous speech of our first president. In an unobtrusive corner was to be found the name of the guest. The table napkins were folded in cocked hat fashion, and everywhere about the table were set glass dishes holding candied cherries in all sorts of guise, cut in halves and placed on top of chocolate drops, dipped whole in scarlet fondant, or oozing with syrup in tiny lace paper cases. The cakes were made hatchet fashion and iced red, white and blue.

There was one magnificent birthday cake with a garland of candied cherries and green leaves (cut from angelica) set into the white icing. The ice cream, from the hands of a clever caterer, was molded into Bunker Hill monument shapes, into hatchets, cocked hats, flags or an enormous two-leaved cherry. To the handles of sherbet cups were sewed tiny silk flags, and in these was served the first course, a delicious fruit salad concocted from oranges, pineapple and white grapes, with maraschino cherries as a garnish. Tomato bouillon followed in quaint blue and white cups; then came cold chicken sliced, peas in timbale cases and creamed potato.

Celery salad with a garnish of red beets was the next course, then the dessert, with cakes and coffee.

While each course was being removed, the girls joined in singing a verse or two from patriotic songs. Over coffee, nuts and candy, the sentiments were read from the place cards and a few five-minute speeches were made by the best talkers at the table. The last ceremony consisted in a smart tweak at the ribbon beside the plate of each guest. This served to bring away from the tree one of the tissue paper cherries, in the heart of which was something which betokened one's future; a thimble, a ring, or the button of the lonely bachelor maid. The last hour spent in the parlors was a complete surprise to the girl household, for within shut doors during the afternoon the teachers had transformed a modern interior into an old-fashioned one, with ancient furniture, queer yellowed prints and quaint portraits on the walls. There were wax flowers, antique china, old samplers, faded embroideries, funny daguerreotypes, ancient silver, beaded reticules, and old books scattered about on tables, lit by tall bayberry candles in brass candlesticks or lamps at which sparkled scores of cut glass danglers. The last part of the evening was as delightful as the supper.

A ST. PATRICK'S DAY PARTY

By Katherine A. Chandler

Send the invitation in the brogue, with which Mr. Dooley and Seumas MacManus are making us familiar, on a paper cut like a shamrock leaf and shaded a delicate green. The answers will probably be worth pinning up for all the guests to enjoy. Decorate with green, having the harp and the shamrock in evidence. Portieres of smilax have a pleasing effect. In one corner have a Blarney stone. All must kiss this the first thing so as to honey their tongues. It should be elevated a little so that they will have to climb up to kiss it.

From the Blarney stone, the guests will pass to a booth to pay their respects to Meave, the ancient Irish queen who has evolved into the Queen Mab of the poets. As they bow low before her, she will pin on each one's back a card bearing an Irish name, which he is to hold during the evening. Then the courtier will rise, receive a bunch of shamrock as a token of Meave's favor, and pass among the other guests to try to discover his own identity. No one is allowed to take the card off, but must learn who he is by questioning. The names may be of real or fictitious persons, and of Irish birth or descent, such as Kathleen Mavourneen, Kathleen Aroon, Norah Creina, Thomas Moore, Robert Emmet, President McKinley, General Sheridan. If possible secure a harpist; if not, have any instrument and some of the sweet old Irish songs, as: The Harp That Once Through Tara's Halls, The Wearing of the Green, Kathleen Mavourneen, Kathleen Aroon, The Last Rose of Summer, etc. All present should join the singing. For refreshments, have pistachio cream and "shamrock" cakes. These can be easily made by getting a clover shape at the tinner's; insert a piece of citron for a stem

and coat with an icing tinted with a green vegetable
coloring matter. If something warm is desired, an
oyster stew may be substituted for the "Irish stew," hot
baked Irish potatoes in their jackets and "a cup of tay."

AN APRIL FOOL'S EVENING

By Marjorie March

The would-be hostess has a smile and a big interro-
gation mark for my greeting as I write of this occasion. "It must be a very informal evening," I avow;
"both inclination and purse say so." And she nods
in response. So let us imagine we have invited
twenty-five guests, all well known to each other, and the
invitations we must word somewhat in this way:

Miss Blank:
   The pleasure of your company is requested at an
informal April Fool's party, from eight until twelve,
April first. Please wear sheet and pillowcase dress.

Yours very sincerely, B——.

The designs of sheet and pillowcase dresses are
endless, and the whole effect is rather pretty and ghostlike as the guests assemble in the parlor ready for the
fun. The host and hostess should be similarly clad, but
to distinguish them, they might have tiny bells sewed
to their disguise that "they may make music wherever
they go." Red jesters' caps generously supplied with
bells are a good addition and make attractive souvenirs
for the guests to take home. These may or may not be

supplied to the guests in the dressing room. It is a little additional trouble in preparation of the evening.

When all are assembled the April Fools' dance begins. All the ghostlike figures range themselves in line. One person at a time steps out of the rank, whispers his or her name to the hostess, who with paper and pencil in hand is to be score keeper, and she writes down his guesswork. He is to guess without touching the figures who each person is, saying the guess out loud that all may hear. If the guess is right the ghostlike personator guessed keeps silent—if the guesser makes a mistake, the figure before him calls out "April Fool," the score keeper, as I said, keeping track of the number of times he is fooled. At the end of the line being reached, a gay waltz strikes up from the piano. The sheeted figures seize each other as partners until the music suddenly ceases once more and the "ghosts" line up for another guesser. This does away with any advantage the last guesser might have over the first in being April Fooled. And so the merriment waxes loud until all have guessed and the hostess orders the masks removed and announces the name of the guesser who was April Fooled the least. A prize should be given to the most successful. This game is new and is great fun, as can be imagined.

The next part of the program as announced by the hostess is the finding of tiny bells hidden here and there and everywhere. The one who finds the greatest number of bells is to be proclaimed chief jester and will have the honor of cutting the April Fool pie at the supper table. This game scatters the guests and for fifteen minutes gives chances for charming tete-a-tetes and whispered conferences in corners, that makes the evening pleasant and keeps the merriment afloat. When the name of the chief jester is announced, the party disappears into the dining room. Here the guests are served at small tables, all the viands, however, being placed on the center table. The April Fool pie causes much fun. This should be an enormous pie of pie-crust filled with tiny trifles wrapped in tissue paper. On the top of the pie twenty-four little birds cut out of black paper are perched by means of pins stuck through their feet. Also pinned to the pie is this verse:

> When this pie is opened,
>   The birds begin to sing?
> That is where you're April Fooled.
>   We won't do such a thing!

As I said, the pie can hold any tiny trinkets. If some personal joke can be carried out by the character of the gifts, so much the better. If one wishes to be at the trouble of having bells (little ones, of course) stitched here and there and everywhere, it is a carrying out of the idea that a fool must have cap and bells. A fringe of bells to the tablecloths, as an edge to the candle shades, and on the rungs of the chairs, would be the most effective and best spots.

Fried oysters, with sandwiches and coffee, ices and cakes, would make a good menu. Here there should be no fooling. The candies that are made of cotton, the food that is deluged with pepper, etc., etc., seem but poor jokes to the average jester, and when hospitality is to play the fool it would be the hight of rudeness to his guests.

CHURCH AFFAIRS

CHURCH AFFAIRS

THE STRAWBERRY FESTIVAL

By Annabel Lee

THE month of June is the accepted time for the strawberry festival, which furnishes an excuse for a church fair or for a money-raising device, under a new name and with fresh attractions. The ideal arrangement is to have the festival out of doors, making it as summery as possible. But alas, in the north Dame Nature is a capricious person, even in June, and it is a trifle risky to plan for an outdoor fete. However, let us appoint the night when there is to be a moon, and let us suppose that some generous soul has been found who possesses a spacious shady lawn and a roomy house with verandas, and who is willing to sacrifice her family, her possessions and herself, particularly her temper, to the good of the cause for which the festival is given. Let a committee of capable workers, not shirkers, be selected to manage the affair, conferring with the owner of the house, but not exacting much of her. It is enough to loan a house and grounds, to prepare them for the event, and to set them in order afterward without having the actual responsibility.

In the first place arrange round or square tables, seating six or eight persons, over the lawn and verandas.

The veranda tables will appeal to the people who prefer to "keep off the grass." Use fine white linen tablecloths and have for centerpieces small ferns stuck into tins of wet moss or sand, or if some gardener will allow his strawberry patch to be rifled, use blossoms and leaves. Failing to get either ferns or strawberry flowers, use June roses of a deep pink tint.

If table dishes are hired, have white, or pink and white, trying to keep the arrangement of color in strawberry red, green and white. Folded Japanese paper napkins of white, or white bordered with strawberry flowers or berries, should be laid at each plate, with knife, folk, spoon and glass. Have no food except relishes on the table, and serve each order separately. Nothing so spoils the appearance of a table as a mixture of half-filled dishes, and it spoils the appetite, too. Have each table in charge of a matron with two waitresses, the prettiest girls to be found, and ask them to dress in white. The matron will see that the table is kept in order and the girls will wait upon the patrons of the feast.

Place some rugs and easy chairs in sheltered spots to attract the people who do not care to stroll about the grounds, and have rustic benches cozily located in the garden for tete-a-tetes. Use plenty of Japanese lanterns for decoration, but depend for light (which will not fail) upon large headlights or lanterns with reflectors, hung on convenient trees. A few large tables covered with white paper and sheltered from view by screens might be placed in the background for serving the supper, or the food might be brought from the kitchen—whichever plan seemed most convenient. A sales table for the display of aprons, embroidery and bags of various kinds might be included in the arrangements. However, for an out-of-door party it seems hardly desirable to offer anything for sale except the supper, which should be the main feature, and beyond reproach. The very best cooks should be asked to provide the food and great care taken to have everything as dainty and attractive as possible; hence all details must be carefully planned and arrangements made in advance. No eleventh hour haste will atone for first hour delay.

In a conspicuous place set a table holding a glass bowl of strawberry frappe or lemonade, to be served in small glass cups. A block of ice hollowed out, with a lighted pink candle inside, may be put in the center of the bowl, and the frappe heaped around the ice, insuring coolness. Decorate the table with strawberry vines or ferns, and have two white-robed maidens to serve the frappe.

The supper may be served from five to eight o'clock, as June evenings have long, delightful twilight, and the lanterns need not be lighted early. Music is an attraction to such a festival, but an orchestra adds to the expense, and it might be inadvisable to hire one. A street piano (at proper distance) might create amusement and add a novel feature, or perhaps some amateur performers on mandolin, banjo and guitar might be induced, in other words, coaxed, to volunteer their services. Such an offer must be taken up at once, giving no one time to change his mind.

Now, for the supper. It must be hearty, but not heavy, for rich food in summer is unnecessary; it must be varied to suit different tastes, and yet be made up of articles which may be served cold and which will not spoil quickly.

Lobster salad makes an appetizing dish, perfect in color, to serve for such a supper; but direful tales are told of the effect of combining lobster, strawberries and ice cream, so, to keep temptation from the injudicious, lobster salad must be tabooed. Cold boiled ham and tongue thinly sliced and garnished with parsley will answer for meats. Tomatoes cut in halves and served on a leaf of crisp lettuce with a spoonful of golden mayonnaise, will furnish a tempting salad. Saratoga potatoes, radishes, pickles and pimolas will add zest to the supper. Individual sweet shortcakes, strawberries, the very choicest, and cream, rich and yellow, strawberry ice cream, strawberry eclairs, sponge cake, angel cake, small cakes, make a list of sweets to suit each and all, while coffee and chocolate will serve for beverages.

It is a good plan to order the rolls from some well-known bakery and have them delivered fresh just before the supper. The butter may be served in pats if anyone has the patience to roll them. Cakes marked in tiny squares can be bought and cut deftly, and kept on ice. A pretty menu card should be placed on each table, and the supper may be served *a la carte* or for a fixed price, with ice cream and strawberries extra. With plenty of help in the kitchen and a well-defined plan of service, this supper should be easy to provide, and would surely prove attractive if well advertised.

The same plan might be carried out on a church lawn if the situation was suitable. Yet it is a noticeable fact that an entertainment which is given on private grounds draws more people and seems to be a trifle more novel and attractive.

The rolls, crackers, Saratoga potatoes, radishes, pimolas, strawberries, cream, ice cream, frappe, small cakes and angel cake may be purchased from the baker and grocer; all the other dishes on the menu should be homemade. If enough money can be raised beforehand to pay for the food purchased, so much the better for the profits from the supper.

After all the arrangements have been made, the Weather, with a big W, may interfere at the very last, and a flight indoors be necessary, or a postponement may seem the wisest plan. It requires abundant courage to undertake an out-of-door party, yet when everything is favorable success is unquestioned.

FOR AN INDOOR FESTIVAL

An indoor festival is not dependent upon smiling skies, and may be planned with full security and confidence. Church parlors and kitchen will provide the necessary room and permit more elaborate features in the shape of a bazar. A novelty in a sales table is a large round table decorated to resemble a wheel, with a mound of strawberries surrounded with green leaves for the hub, and radiating spokes made of long strips of smilax, trailing fern or vines. In the intervening spaces have jars of rich strawberry preserve, jelly and jam for sale, made by housewives whose work can be recommended. At a food sale the question is often asked: "Who made this?" And if in reply one can say: "Mrs. X, who makes delicious preserves," a sale is effected at once on the strength of a reputation. A newspaper article on food adulteration tells of strawberry (?) jam made out of glucose, coloring matter and seeds of timothy grass. None of those delicacies enter into homemade productions, which always command a high price.

A table for the sale of homemade cake and cookies is a fitting companion to the preserve table. Decorate a table for candy with green and strawberry red on a white cloth, using red and green crepe paper and silver candelabra, with red candles and shades. Have homemade candy in glass dishes; also salted almonds and stuffed dates; these will bring a good sum of money. Scales, white paper bags and boxes and red twine should be provided for packing up the candy.

The crepe papers may be purchased at the stationer's store in a bewildering variety of colors and patterns. This paper is most useful for decoration, and skillful fingers make from it bewitching lamp and candle shades, boxes, patty cases, flowers and paper dolls, which cost little and find ready purchasers. Wall paper in artistic flower patterns makes attractive covers for all kinds of boxes, large and small. It also makes dainty photograph frames when skillfully mounted with pasteboard, glass and passepartout. A paper table might include stationery, photographs and writing tablets.

June roses vie with strawberries in rich reds, and may be used in decoration, or sold at a flower booth. The frappe or lemonade table should have a place of honor; if space permits the storage of a freezer full of vanilla ice cream (out of sight), strawberry college ice may be served at this table, with a spoonful of ice cream covered with a spoonful of crushed strawberries, sweetened with boiled sugar syrup, in tall, bell-shaped glasses. The supper tables should be arranged as for the outdoor festival and the same supper served.

STRAWBERRY FESTIVAL MENU

Cold ham   Cold tongue   Rolls
Saratoga potatoes   Tomato salad   Crackers
Pickles   Radishes   Pimolas
Individual sweet shortcakes   Strawberries and cream
Strawberry ice cream   Strawberry eclairs
Sponge cake   Angel cake   Small cakes
Coffee   Chocolate

A few recipes for cakes and preserves may help in preparing the supper and sale:

Individual Sweet Shortcakes—Beat three eggs light, add one cupful of fine granulated sugar, and beat again.

Add one cupful of sifted flour mixed with one teaspoonful of cream of tartar and one-half teaspoonful of soda. Add three tablespoonfuls of milk. Beat well and bake in slightly buttered cupcake tins in a quick oven. When cold remove the centers and fill the cases with crushed sweetened strawberries and cover with sweetened whipped cream. These cakes are much better to serve for a supper than the usual shortcake, which needs to be eaten as soon as it is baked. A cold, soggy shortcake is a dish to avoid.

Strawberry Eclairs—Boil together in a saucepan one cupful of boiling water, one-fourth cupful of butter and a speck of salt. As it begins to boil, stir in one cupful of sifted flour. Stir constantly until the mixture leaves the sides of the pan and cleaves together in a ball. When partly cool add four eggs, beating them in one at a time. Drop carefully in long narrow strips, some distance apart, on buttered tins, and bake in a moderate oven until well risen—about thirty minutes. Leave the oven door open a few minutes before removing the eclairs, to prevent their falling. When they are cool split one side, fill with sweetened strawberries or jam. Spread with boiled icing colored with strawberry juice.

Canned Strawberries—Hull and wash perfect fruit and pack it into jars. To each quart allow one-half pound of sugar and one cupful of water. Boil this into a syrup and fill each jar two-thirds full. Screw on the covers loosely, place the jars on a rack in a boiler two-thirds full of tepid water. Cover, and when the water boils allow twelve minutes' cooking. Remove the jars to a table, fill them brimming full with hot syrup. Put on the rubbers and screw on the covers firmly.

Preserved Strawberries—Hull and wash the fruit. Allow three-fourths pound of sugar to one pound of fruit. Place the berries and sugar in layers in a large porcelain bowl and let it stand over night. In the morning drain off the juice and heat it in a preserving kettle, letting it boil for fifteen minutes. Then add the fruit and when it boils skim if necessary and fill into hot jars, sealing them closely. A thicker preserve or jam is made by allowing one pound of sugar to each pound of fruit and boiling from twenty to thirty minutes and storing in glasses, like jelly.

Strawberry Jelly—Select perfect fruit, firm and even in size. Lay aside the best, about half, and press the juice from the rest. Strain, and to each pound (pint) of juice allow one pound of sugar and boil fully twenty minutes. Weigh the selected fruit and add an equal quantity of sugar. Add to the jelly and boil carefully a few minutes. No exact time can be given. Try a little in a saucer and when the jelly seems thick and firm pour it into glasses. Seal when cold. This is not a very firm jelly, but is delicious.—American Kitchen Magazine.

Sunshine Strawberries—Select dark colored fruit. Cook three pounds of fine granulated sugar with two cupfuls of boiling water without stirring, till a thread will spin when the syrup is dropped from a spoon. Cook the berries in this syrup for fifteen minutes after they

begin to boil.   Pour the preserve on large platters, cover
with gauze and let it stand in the sun for two or more
days until very thick.   Store in glasses and cover with
a paper.—Boston Cooking School.

Strawberry Sherbet—Use one quart of berry juice,
four cupfuls of sugar, the juice of two lemons, three
pints of water and a few whole strawberries.   Serve in
a punch bowl with a block of ice, or freeze for frappe.

A CHURCH SUPPER

By Mrs. A. R.

The annual pay supper of the women's missionary
society of our church has always been a trial and a
vexation, until affairs reached a climax.   The crowd
was large and unruly, and the disgraceful spectacle was
witnessed of newcomers standing behind the chairs of
those who were seated and clamoring for haste on the
part of the diners.   In this rush the diners were poorly
served, the tables soon lost all semblance of daintiness,
the waste of food was outrageous and toilets and tempers suffered.   A radical change was decided upon and
the sequel proves the plan a success.   We arranged four
long tables in the hall where the supper was served,
each table capable of accommodating fifty.   When the
first fifty people had lined up in the anteroom for their
supper, they were admitted to Table No. 1, and the
doorkeeper was instructed to prevent any further entries.
The fifty were daintily served with oyster stew, crackers, pickles, celery, rolls and butter, and for this first

course in the menu, one coupon from tickets was detached. At the end of seven minutes a gong sounded and the first fifty diners advanced decently and in order to Table No. 2. In three minutes Table No. 1 was brushed and reset and the second installment of fifty from the anteroom was admitted and received exactly the same treatment as the first fifty. The few in the anteroom who were in excess of fifty awaited without grumbling, secure in the knowledge that in ten minutes their turn would come. At Table No. 2, the menu was Boston baked beans, pickled cabbage, brown bread, salad and preserves, and a second coupon was detached. At the end of seven minutes the gong sounded again and the first fifty advanced to Table No. 3, and those at Table No. 1 advanced to Table No. 2. Three minutes were devoted to brushing and resetting the tables, and then the third installment of fifty was admitted from the anteroom to Table No. 1. At Table No. 3, the menu included turkey and all its accompaniments, mashed potatoes, cranberry sauce, slaw, olives and hot biscuit and butter, coffee and doughnuts, and a third coupon was detached. At the end of seven minutes, the diners advanced once more, the first fifty (or as many as desired of this number) to Table No. 4. Table No. 4 was known as an "extra," and to this only holders of "four-coupon" tickets were privileged. At Table No. 4, ice cream, cake, fruits and confectionery were served. Those who did not desire the extra quietly passed from the supper room. This supper, as stated, proved a success. At no time was there a clamoring crowd in the anteroom. At the tables the diners shared exactly alike and were served simultaneously. The business man with scant time at his disposal secured an ample meal within half an hour, and above all there was no waste of food. Each plate was set before the diner with an impartial and amply sufficient allotment of food, and in almost every case the plate was cleared. Late in the evening as the diners decreased in number, they were admitted in squads of twenty-five and even a lesser number. But the idea of progression was rigidly maintained throughout. We sold our "four-coupon" tickets for fifty cents and the "three-coupon" tickets for thirty-five cents.

A CHARITY POST BOX

By Mary Dawson

A charity fair in the south brought out some fresh ways of drawing in the dimes and dollars for a good cause. One clever little idea took the form of a post box, a wee booth fitted up with a window at either side where letters were sold for charity. A pretty girl acted as postmistress. From one side she delivered the men's letters, from the reverse side those of the women. Anyone paying a quarter received a letter. In the men's side the mail was prepared by the girls of the neighborhood. The girls' side was fitted out by the men. The envelopes were addressed simply "To the Charitable." Sometimes they contained lively little letters; others revealed a laughable verse or a sketch or a camera snapshot. In every case the communication was signed with the name of the correspondent, author, artist or photographer, as the case might be. The price for each envelope was twenty-five cents, irrespective of the contents. As it was known that each popular man and girl in the neighborhood had contributed at least once, and often as many as six times, the box was constantly surrounded by eager venturers desirous of obtaining a souvenir from the pen of a certain man or a certain girl. Reckless plungers invested half a dozen times before the desired memento was secured. Within two hours' time the postmistress was obliged to confess that "all mail had been distributed."

FOR THE SUNDAY SCHOOL

By G. F. S.

A pretty entertainment was planned and carried out for fifteen Sunday school pupils by a teacher at the church parlors. Small paper and envelopes were used for the invitations, which ran like this: "Miss S. S. will entertain her Sunday school class at the church parlors Saturday afternoon at 2.30 o'clock. You are invited to this peanut party." The scholars (all girls in this case) were prompt, and on the arrival of the fifteen were told to find the peanuts. After a successful hunt, they were allowed to eat them at the kindergarten tables, and while they were eating, the teacher prepared the peanut race. Rows of peanuts, seven in a row, were placed on the floor, knives were given to the girls, and the fun began. The peanuts must be carried on the knife to a basket, and so on, one by one, till the girl whose row was done first secured the prize, a box of peanut candy. Next chairs were placed in a row, one ready to sit in, the next back to front, and so on alternately; seven peanuts were placed in each of the fifteen chairs. The scholars marched around the chairs to the sound of music and as the teacher stopped, grabbed a peanut from the front of a chair, and so on. Sometimes the teacher stopped playing quickly, sometimes there was a longer march; they never knew just when the music would cease. At the close, the girl having the most peanuts received a box of peanut fudge, and the others were allowed to eat their captures. For the next and last amusement, the scholars stood in two rows opposite one another, the teacher joining the game that there might be eight on a side. A basket of ten peanuts was placed at the head of each row; at the word "go," the leader bent, took up one peanut, passed it to second, who passed it to third and so on, the leader meanwhile having picked up another and passed it on. No girl was allowed to have more than one peanut in her hands at one time. The row that won received all the peanuts, to be eaten by them. At the kindergarten tables refreshments were passed, consisting of sandwiches, pickles, peanut cheeseballs, frosted cookies, small round sugared doughnuts, chocolate and cocoanut cake.

SUNDAY HOURS

By H. C. C.

With a gathering of children whose intentions for spending Sunday had been defeated by bad weather, the following impromptu amusement proved most successful:

For the foundation of play, take one of the interesting tales of the Old Testament. Read this story to the child audience, abridging it as much as possible, so they will get merely the simple lines of the tale. After apportioning to each child one character or several unimportant ones, to be represented by paper figures cut from old magazines, set the scene and begin the play. The children will be intensely interested in providing proper figures, such as a baby Moses for Pharaoh's daughter to find, a suitable young man for Joseph, a harp for the young David. Indeed, there is as much entertainment and instruction in the mere getting ready as in the play itself. Then there are accessories for the scene to be found and arranged, all of which the boys will furnish with enthusiasm. For the movement of the play again read the tale aloud, and each child will carry his paper figure through the neccessary performance.

This game possesses so much of charm that, in one household at least, it closes with an excitement like that experienced in reading a story "to be continued," at the most thrilling point. It makes our little folks' conceptions of the life of the "chosen people" more definite.

The table with embroidered doilies and white chrysanthemums

SUPPERS AND A FAGOT PARTY

By Linda Hall Larned

A group of social lights decided last Thanksgiving to have a series of suppers conducted upon the same lines as the beloved dinner dance of a decade ago. The result was really delightful—suppers of six at five different houses at which the courses were limited to four The brief supper was chosen as being easy to prepare, and one of the guests opened her house, a large colonial one, for the fagot party which was the wind-up.

One supper was served on a round mahogany table with embroidered doilies and white chrysanthemums for decoration. A centerpiece of silver and glass filled with the flowers was surrounded by six crystal candlesticks in which were yellow fluted candles. These were held in by a circle of chrysanthemums in shallow tin receptacles about an inch and a half wide, which are made in sections to be adjusted to any table.

The fagot party was a gathering of this merry crowd around a big fireplace, a veritable ingle nook in which there were arrangements for a real fire of wood. To every guest was given a small bunch of fagots to burn, and as each guest was called up to replenish the fire he began his "stunt" with the first twig laid on and did not finish until the last one was in ashes. The actor who succeeded best in amusing the audience received a prize and the one who failed, a consolation. One person gave a clever imitation of Mr. Dooley and his impression of the St. Louis convention, even to the Bryan weep. Then some nimble dame gave a Loie Fuller skirt dance with the aid of a voluminous Mother Hubbard of pink cheesecloth prepared and donned for the occasion. Another told a story of real adventure which was both amusing and pathetic, and still another gave a fair representation of a folk-lore story teller. A ventriloquist and prestidigitator kept the audience amused, and then a beautiful voice was heard in the gamut of songs, from In the Garden of Sleep to Bedelia.

The enjoyment culminated with the refreshments, consisting of a large bowl of mulled cider on a huge silver tray. The bowls were brought in on another tray and so were sandwiches and crullers. The cider was "mulled" after the following recipe: To one quart of cider, add one teaspoon of whole spice and a half teaspoon of cassia buds, boil three minutes, add three eggs beaten thoroughly and serve at once. This amount would serve six persons. On the tray surrounding the bowl were dozens of burning "snapdragons." These were large plumped raisins soaked in alcohol. They were set on fire before the attention of the company was called, and then each guest was given a small bowl and told to "snap" as many dragons as he or she could into the bowl while they were still burning. This is easier than it seems, as the burning alcohol will not harm the fingers. Each one's bowl was examined and the one having the most received the prize. Then the hot cider was poured into the bowl, the raisins adding to the flavor.